Who Are The Sons of the Promise?

WRITTEN BY
Don Reed

Unless otherwise indicated, all scripture references are from the King James Version of the Bible

Who are the Sons of the Promise?
Don Reed

ISBN 978-1-4507-0078-8

All rights reserved. Reproduction of contents and/or cover in whole or part without written permission is prohibited.

Cover Design by Margo Bush

Published by Bush Publishing
P.O. Box 692082 Tulsa, OK 74169
www.WeDoBooksNow.com

Printed in the USA

About the Author

Pastor Don Reed, second-generation preacher, was taught the Holy way by Emery and Lorene Reed and a very godly grandmother, Ella Hieronymus. He was raised in Osage County, Oklahoma. He is married to the lovely Navada Faye Ross Reed. God blessed the union with two special sons, Jerry and Mike Reed, and families.

We have pastored and evangelized for over 50 years. In addition to this book, I wrote a manual on Revelation. We have been privileged to make four trips to Africa preaching and teaching the Word of God. We presently have six grandchildren and eight great-grandchildren.

Looking back at our fifty years of working in the Lord's vineyard, all of our pastoral work has been in Oklahoma. Our first church was in a little town in Hughes County, Calvin's, which was our first love as pastors. Only eternity will reveal the great trophies so dear to our hearts that we found in that little town.

Our second church was in Holdenville with dear friends. We then moved to Cushing, which left us with fond memories. Then we moved on to pastor in Bartlesville and enjoyed God's anointing on our work there. The next twelve years of our labor we spent in Sand Springs. We were privileged to build a new church with a host of friends. Our two sons were married while we were there, and we stepped into the role of grandparents.

For the last 24 years we have pastored in Ft. Gibson, and again we were privileged to build another new church. Ft. Gibson has enriched our lives. We have also been blessed to make four trips teaching and preaching in Uganda, Africa.

We are a blessed family. I trust this book will be a blessing to you and yours.

Dedication

I dedicate this book to three very special people, my lovely wife of over 50 years, who has been more than a helpmate. Without her, our ministry could not have been. I'm indebted to the Lord for picking her out and preparing her for our ministry. Our journey has been greater than I could have ever imagined.

Then to Richard and Kathy Chandler. Without this couple and their hard work, and their love for the Word of God, this book would not have been. This book is actually a series of Sunday School lessons I taught. The Chandlers recorded and brought it to where it is now. God will bless them eternally, and they will have a part in every soul that is blessed hereby.

Foreword

As Paul wrote the book of Hebrews, he gave a clear picture of how we are benefited today, and showed it to us in the tabernacle and all things there related. It is likened unto the Lord wanting us to receive the greater benefits that are in the promises of God. He shows us these truths in the life of Abraham. As we study his life carefully, we will better understand the many promises that God has made for you and me.

Come walk with us through the life of Abraham and therein we can reach a greater order of excellency. The word Hebrew was a name given to Abraham by the Canaanites, which simply means "a man from beyond the river." Let us go in search of that man from beyond the river, and may your name inspire the coming generations, as does his.

In searching for this man, there are many great truths God would have to enrich our lives. God is a covenant keeping God. If we can better understand that the covenant God has extended to us, then you and yours will be made recipients of the promises that are eternal. Our horizons will not just be earthly, but eternal.

The Lord said through the mouth of Isaiah in Isaiah 59:20,21, the Redeemer shall come to Zion and this is my Covenant with them saith the Lord. My spirit which I have put in thy mouth shall not depart out of thy mouth nor out of the mouth of thy seed, nor out of the mouth of thy seeds, seed, saith the Lord from henceforth and forever.

In Acts 2:17 and it shall come to pass in the last days, saith the Lord, I will pour out of my spirit upon all flesh and your sons and your daughters shall prophesy and your young men shall see visions and your old men shall dream dreams. And in verse 18 it will go out of our house to those about us. So let us search diligently and let us make sufficient commitments of obedience that we shall take a multitude with us from this life into that eternal day.

I trust your search will be a success.

TABLE OF CONTENTS

Introduction
Every Man That Hath Heard..................................1
The Call of Abram..11
Abram's Altars..20
Abram's Sacrifice..30
Abram & The Church...39
Abram & Abraham..47
Abraham & Predestination..................................57
Abraham – A Servant's Heart..............................65
Abraham with Justice & Judgments....................75
The Sodomy of Sodom..82
Lot Lingered & Lot's Salvation............................93
Abraham & Abimelech.......................................103
Abraham – Father of the Promise.....................112
Abraham's Covenant of Covenants...................123
Three Days Journey..132
Mountain of Moriah...142
Thou Hast Obeyed My Voice.............................150
Lineage & Bloodline of Abraham......................157
Abraham & Eliezer...166
Sarah's Tent..176

Introduction

This study is about the promise God gave Abram. We must understand and establish the promise and know that anyone who believes Jesus is our Savior is a child of the promise.

In order to receive the great blessings of God for us and our families, we must understand what the promise is. To understand the promise, we must study Abram's life and the events that transpired. Who received the promise and how? How was it kept or lost? We must go back and establish the promise to insure that we are seed of the promise. I believe there is more for us in the kingdom of Heaven than we have received thus far.

I want to share with you what God has revealed to me over the years about being a child of the promise. I want you to receive the great blessings of God for you and your family. As I've studied the book of Revelation, I've learned I must return to Genesis to confirm every subject. This study is about the promise God gave Abram, so we must understand his life.

Jesus said, "Go preach, the kingdom is at hand." We can reach it but we must know what we are reaching for. If we have faith, everything is within our reach. We are heirs and joint-heirs, but we must live righteous and obedient lives.

Every Man That Hath Heard!

Scripture references:
John 6:45	Acts 2:47
Luke 16:23	Ephesians 4:11,12
Luke 4:18,21	Hebrews 11:35
John 20:17	Revelations 2:7,11,17,29
John 17:12	Revelations 3:13,22

If we hear what the Word of God is saying to us, we might understand that we are the sons of God that His life is our light, and that light shines in our pathway, that we might become as He is.

Ephesians 4:11-12 And He gave some, apostles; and some prophets; and some, evangelists; and some pastors and teachers. For the perfecting of the saints, for the work of the ministry, for the edifying of the body of Christ.

Paul makes this observation, that when Jesus ascended up on high, He gave gifts unto men. What that is simply saying is that, when Jesus came forth out of the sepulcher and as He was leading the captivity captive, he stopped off, by the way of the earth. In other words, when he spent the three days ministering in the regions of the damned. He was giving opportunity to those who had never heard and never knew. He was not preaching to those who knew and turned it down. He was speaking to those who did not know and had not heard.

Therefore, as we study the Word of God, let us be one of those who have heard, so we will be one of those who know.

John 6:45 It is written in the prophets, And they shall be all taught of God. Every man therefore that hath heard, and hath learned of the Father, cometh unto me.

As Jesus led the captivity captive, He changed the location of those who even died in the faith, prior to His ascension and resurrection. The righteous dead or the believing dead was referred to as down. Now after this event they were never referred to again as down but rather up.

Luke 16:23 And in hell he lift up his eyes, being in torments, and seeth Abraham afar off and Lazarus in his bosom.

In hell, the rich man lifted up his eyes and saw up yonder, Abraham and Lazarus.

As Jesus left the regions of the damned and headed to Heaven to apply His blood on the mercy seat of Glory, He stopped off by way of the earth. Many things tell us that. For example, when Mary met Him at the sepulcher, she ran up to embrace him, and He said:

John 20:17 Touch me not, for I am not yet ascended to my Father: but go to my brethren and say unto them, I ascend unto my Father and your Father, and to my God and your God.

Now this was on the resurrection morning, so we know that He had not ascended from the cross up; He descended from the cross down, taking the keys of death, hell, and the grave away from the adversary. Now He is on his way up and Ephesians tells us that He stopped by and gave gifts unto men. In Ephesians, Paul talks about the apostles, prophets, evangelists, pastors, teachers, whom Jesus gave to the Church for the edifying of the saints.

Therefore, we have two great fronts:

• To reach the lost and the edifying of the saints, preparing them for the second coming of Jesus Christ!

Jesus gave great gifts unto men. Not only did He give

those gifts to us, but we need to understand that someone who is gifted to help us has received a gift from God. That means your ministry is a God given-gift, and nothing in this world takes priority over that gift that God has given you. Therefore, what you can do for God is greater than anything else that could have been given to you, because God, who created all things, gave it to you.

His gift is of great importance and value. That is why He gave some apostles, prophets, evangelist, pastors and teachers, but mainly teachers, because we feel that we are all teachers. Because the bigger percent of all people who are won to the Lord are not won because of a sermon or song, but of a life that was lived.

These ministry gifts Godly influence us, teach us, and touch our lives. The gifts are for the edifying of the saints and the preparing of a people until we all come into the full measure and statue of Jesus Christ. We all have been predestinated to come into the fullness of Christ and then we are going to be as He was. Now that does not mean we walk around as lords, but to be humble Christians who have received the anointing of God, to perform the ministry that has been given unto us, each one gifted and anointed for that ministry. When Jesus went to the synagogue, He stood and read this scripture.

Luke 4:18,21 The Spirit of the Lord is upon me, Because He hath anointed me to preach the Gospel to the poor; He hath sent me to heal the broken hearted, To preach deliverance to the captives and recovering of sight to the blind, to set at liberty them that are bruised. And he began to say unto them, this day is this scripture fulfilled in your ears.

Jesus put the emphasis on the Holy Ghost, continued reading the scripture, and then sat down. So this is our ministry, your ministry, the thing that God has gifted you to do in the kingdom of God, with the anointing of the

Holy Ghost. Now this is a steppingstone to the next level. Not every person that saw Him, or listened to the words He was speaking, heard Him.

There are many people that do not hear the preachers preach or the teachers teach, because their hearts are not fixed on hearing. In the Book of Revelation, He makes the same statement to every one of the seven churches of Asia.

- Revelations 2:7... <u>Ephesus Church</u>

He that hath an ear, let him hear what the Spirit saith unto the churches; To him that overcometh will I give to eat of the tree of life, which is in the midst of the paradise of God.

- Revelations 2:11... <u>Smyrna Church</u>

He that hath ear, let him hear what the Spirit saith unto the churches;

He that overcometh shall not be hurt by the second death.

- Revelations 2:17... <u>Pergamos Church</u>

He that hath ear, let him hear what the Spirit saith unto the churches; To him that overcometh will I give to eat of the hidden manna and will give him a white stone, and in the stone a new name written, which no man knoweth saving he that receiveth it.

- Revelations 2:26 & 29... <u>Thyatira Church</u>

And he that overcometh, and keepeth my works unto the end, to him will I give power over the nations: he that hath an ear, let him hear what the Spirit saith unto the churches.

- Revelations 3:5 & 6... <u>Sardis Church</u>

He that overcometh, the same shall be clothed in white raiment; and I will not blot out his name out of the Book of Life, but I will confess his name before my Father and before his angels.

He that hath an ear, let him hear what the Spirit saith unto the churches.

• Revelations 3:12 &13... <u>Philadelphia Church</u>

Him that overcometh will I make a pillar in the temple of my God and he shall go no more out: and I will write upon him the name of my God and the name of the city of my God, which is New Jerusalem, which cometh down out of heaven from my God: and I will write upon him my new name.

He that hath an ear, let him hear what the Spirit saith unto the churches.

• Revelations 3:21 & 22... <u>Laodicea Church</u>

To him that overcometh, will I grant to sit with me in my throne, even as I also overcame and am set down with my Father in his throne.

He that hath an ear, let him hear what the Spirit saith unto the churches.

Now in the Church today those of you that hath an ear, hear what the Holy Ghost is saying to the church. Those of you who have an ear to hear, you are blessed. If you really want to know, you are a minority. Now, your mind is only an instrument that is used by the heart.

If your heart is not fixed on hearing, you will find every excuse in the world, not to even be around where the Word is being taught or preached. That is what Jesus is saying in the Gospel of John, every man that heareth.

So the questions we need to ask ourselves is this:

- Am I Listening?
- Am I hearing the preacher?
- Am I hearing the teacher?
- Am I listening with my heart?
- Am I yawning or looking around?
- Am I going through my purse?
- Am I getting up and going to the restroom?
- Am I looking and watching others being disruptive?
- Am I participating in what is being said?
- Am I answering questions that are being asked or thinking about them?
- Am I listening for the answers?

John 6:45 It is written in the prophets, And they shall be all taught of God. Every man therefore that hath heard, and hath learned of the Father, cometh unto me.

Not only have they heard, but have learned from the Father. First, you have to hear, before you can learn. Everyone that hears and learns, comes to Jesus. Those who didn't listen didn't even know who Jesus was when He passed by. Thousands of them said crucify Him; they did not have a clue who they were crucifying. They had not heard and they have not learned, so they crucified Him.

So are we listening?

Is our heart fixed on receiving the Word of God?

How important is this to you and to your family?

This is eternal. Your family, your friends, and everyone that you come together and agree on, can be and shall be saved. How important is that? It is more important than we will ever know until we get to our heavenly home. One soul, one second in hell, is too much.

Jesus, the Son of God did not save everybody that was lost. He did not reach everybody that heard him, and he did not heal everyone that was sick.

He came to the Pool of Bethesda and five porches were filled with crippled folks, and He healed one man. He went to His own city and He healed none, because of their unbelief.

Your sovereignty makes a difference with God and eternity. We decide whether we hear and learn. We decide whether we are made the recipient and receive the knowledge. In receiving the knowledge, we have the power to do greater things in the kingdom of God.

That empowers us to tear down the strong holds of the devil. I want you to notice what Jesus said here: "Now these that have heard, and these that have learned, they will come to Me."

Again, Jesus said in His prayer to the Father before His death:

John 17:12 While I was with them in the world, I kept them in thy name: those that thou gavest me I have kept and none of them is lost, but the son of perdition; that the scripture might be fulfilled.

In other words, Jesus is saying, "Father You did not give Me 5000, You did not give Me 10,000, you gave me 12 apostles." Jesus is making that great prayer to the Father. He is saying He kept all that God had given Him!

Do you understand what Jesus is saying here?

- So by what means and what measure am I given?
- By what means and what measure am I hearing?
- Moreover, what effect does my hearing have to do with who I become?
- How much like Him am I?

Acts 2:47 Praising God and having favor with all the people. And the Lord added to the church daily such as should be saved.

As the church was birthed, there were many being saved.

Why wasn't everyone lost added to the church, why wasn't everyone saved?

He added to the church such as should be saved. There was a reason why they were being saved and a reason why they were not being saved. That is the reason we are looking for.

- Why was it some heard and some did not?
- Why was it some learned and some did not?
- Why was it some were added to the church and some were not?
- Is He a respecter of persons?

Since God is not a respecter of persons, there is a reason why some were saved and others were not. Not everyone running up and down the streets are saved. It is God's will for them to be saved, but why are they not being saved?

Hebrews 11: 35 Women received their dead raised to life again; and others were tortured, not accepting deliverance; that they might obtain a better resurrection:

Who Are the Sons of the Promise?

Some accepted this great miracle working power of God to them personally and to theirs, but others did not. Those who adhered to Christianity were tortured under Nero's rule (60-65 AD). They were fed to lions, wrapped in wax, and burned in the garden. But the Christians knew a better resurrection awaited them.

What is the better resurrection?

The better resurrection is a higher rank in the world to come. If you see this thing in the light of that everything is the same for everybody, then these people died in vain. There was no reason for them to suffer, being sawed asunder and fed to lions. There was no reason for them not to accept deliverance. Nevertheless, they turned it down so they would have a greater reward eternally. Therefore, God added to the church such as should be saved.

I leave you with this question:

Why did he not give Jesus Christ all sinners?

So there is more involved in this than what meets the eye… the sovereignty of man and the power of prayer are greater than we realize.

The Call of Abram

Scripture references:
Genesis 12: 1-2 Now the Lord had said unto Abram, get thee out of thy country and from thy kindred, and from thy father's house unto the land that I will shew thee. And I will make thee a great nation and I will bless thee and make thy name great; and thou shalt be a blessing:

Genesis 12:13   Romans 4:13-17
Genesis 13:12,14,15   2 Corinthians 6:17
Numbers 23:19   Revelation 21:1

    The Old Testament is a schoolmaster to the New Testament. The basic teaching of Christ and the apostles endeavored to substantiate the program and economy of God based on Abraham's covenant. Now we want to make a journey and see the teachings that God has given us, so that we can understand what God really wants to do with His family. We are the family of God. Starting in the life of Abraham, the Hebrews found their name; they were not Hebrews until Abraham. This was the beginning of the Hebrew people. This word "Hebrew" first occurs as given to Abram by the Canaanites in Genesis 14:13. I believe that as we understand what God did for, with, and through Abraham, we will see what God has for our lives, what He wants to do through us, and how we can have the Seeds of the Promise! If we look at where Abraham made the right choices and where his lineage made wrong choices, then you and I can let that be a schoolmaster, so we can make the right choices.

    Abraham naturally started out as Abram in the 11th chapter of Genesis. He does not become Abraham until he has a certain relationship with God, and then God changes his name. For now he is Abram. The name always means much; your name means much and you are identified by

The Call of Abram

your name being called. Not that the name means that, but the structure that you have built will come to mind when your name is mentioned. When your name is called in Heaven, it means something.

Isaiah 66:22 For as the new heavens and the new earth, which I will make, shall remain before me, saith the Lord, so shall your seed and your name remain.

Who was Abraham's father?

Terah

Where did they live?

Ur of the Chaldees near the Euphrates River where the cradle of the human race came from. They were a people who made and worshiped idols. If Terah had not let circumstances in life alter his journey with God, everywhere the name Abraham is mentioned, it would be Terah. Nevertheless, because of some events in life, Terah stopped his journey, stopped his dream, stopped his goal, and sat down.

What were those circumstances?

His son Haran died.

How many sons did Terah have?

Three sons, Haran, Abram and Nahor, but Haran died.

Terah had gone many miles and was headed to Canaan when these circumstances of life came and hindered him. When his son Haran dies, he becomes discouraged an sits down. He said, "The greatest thing I can do now is build a city here and name it after my son Haran, who is deceased."

That is why the Bible says that the word of the Lord came to Abram while he was at Haran. He was at the city were Terah had stopped with his family, sat down, and later died.

Note: Abram's son Haran died in Ur of the Chaldees.

Genesis 12: 1-2 Now the Lord had said unto Abram, get thee out of thy country, and from thy kindred, and from thy father's house unto a land that I will show thee.
And I will make thee a great nation and I will bless thee, and make thy name great; and thou shalt be a blessing.

In essence, the word of the Lord came to Abram saying, "Your daddy has quit the journey, lost his vision, and lost the goal. He has sat down and quit. I want you to pick up and follow Me, and come into the country that I will show thee."

Notice that God is not beating around the bush; He goes straight to the point. He is saying this in simple language: "Abram, you are going to have to get away from your kinfolk, because your kinfolks have caused this thing to stop. You need to get up and get away from them; they are not going any further."

Anytime that you or I say," I know what that means," there is no more room for revelation in that situation. When you say, "I understand what is being said," you do not close the door for understanding and revelation. You may read that scripture over and over, and every time God may give you a different revelation on the same scripture. Keep an appetite for the Word of God, to know more, to do more, and to hear more.

So there came a time God said to Abram, "You cannot stay here and do My will or become what you need to become." That statement is true for each one of us today. God is calling Abram to obedience.

The Call of Abram

When he left Haran, God told him to leave his family. He took with him Lot, his brother-in-law, and that was the first act of disobedience. Abram came out, but he came out with Lot, and he ended up being a liability all the days of their labor.

I thought Lot was Abram's nephew?

Right - Lot was Abram's brother, Haran's son.

I thought Lot was Abram's brother-in-law.

Right- Lot's sister was Sarah (Abram's wife)

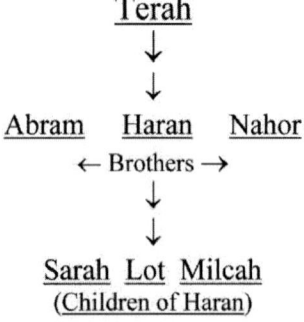

Therefore, Lot is Abram's nephew and brother-in-law also.

Why does Genesis 12:13 say, "I pray thee, thou art my sister"?

In Bible days, they would call kin, sister or brother, if they were of the same bloodline. However, that did not mean that they were in fact brother and sister. So when Abram told the king of Egypt the Sarah was his sister, he was not speaking the whole truth. She was his niece-wife. Therefore, Abram takes with him Lot, his nephew/brother-n-law, and he now has lied to the King of Egypt. If God had not intervened on his behalf, he could have been in real trouble. Now he is humiliated before Pharaoh.

Who Are the Sons of the Promise?

In Genesis chapter 13, Abram returns back from Egypt (a type of sin); he is humiliated, embarrassed, and sent home.

This reminds me of ourselves. Sometimes when we fool around and compromise, we get down in Egypt in sin. We do not belong there, we are not one of them, and we are in the wrong place. We do the wrong thing and we come back embarrassed.

Abram comes back embarrassed, though God continues to bless him.

Now they are coming into the land of Canaan and their herds are too big.

Abram has his herds and Lot has his herds, and they realize that the herds are too big and they need to separate. However, that is not the only reason they need to separate. Abram needs to obey God, leave Egypt, take another step, and separate himself from Lot. Each time these are travailed moments, but they serve as a step in obedience.

So here Abram says to Lot, I have made a mistake in bringing you. That almost always means confusion, and there was great confusion in Abram's camp. When we disobey and fail God, it brings confusion in the home, in our mind, and in every place we turn. So Abram steps up to say to Lot, his brother-in-law, and says, "I have made a mistake; you choose which way you want to go. Whatever way you want to go, I am going the other way." Now remember, Lot can choose for himself which way he wants to go. Lot pitched his tent toward Sodom and chooses the fertile valleys of Sodom. How sad is this?

Genesis 13-12 Abram dwelled in the land of Canaan and Lot swelled in the cities of the plain, and pitched his tent toward Sodom.

The Call of Abram

<u>Sodom:</u>
• Comes from the word "sodomy."
• Perversion is a spiritual sin; it has to do with the promise of the seed.
Rejection of God and His plan for the family…male and female.
• Men are rejecting manhood and their responsibilities. They want to act like women.
• Women want to look like, act like, and be the man. They want to be the head and the boss.

We are not born perverted, we are born with a weakness of principles that can be unto the third and fourth generations, each one weaker and weaker. If the principles are not there in dad and weaker in the son and still weaker in the next one, soon they will be saying that I was born this way.

It is a spiritual sin…. Why?

Because His Word is the seed, it is the Word of God, the Bible. We hide the Word of God in our hearts, and then one day at the altar, we turn and hand him back a son of His own kind. Therefore, perversion is a spiritual sin, because the seed is no longer there, planted as God ordained in the beginning.

There is one more step that is further away from God than sodomy – it is witchcraft. In the Bible, a man brought his son to the disciples and said that his son was a lunatic, and it cast him into the fire. Our sons are Lunatics (that word comes from "lunar").

Now we call in and get our readings, our psychic forecast, our Ouija boards, and our horoscopes. This is the next step away from God.

Sodomy takes the principles of God away from us, and witchcraft or demon possession takes away the mind.

Who Are the Sons of the Promise?

We are no longer human beings but act like animals – we have lost reasoning, we are driven by the devil, like the lunar son. That lunatic will put you in the fire!

Genesis 13: 14-15 And the Lord said unto Abram, after that Lot was separated from him. Lift up thine eyes, and look from the place where thou art northward and southward and eastward and westward:

For all the land which thou seest, to thee will I give it, and to thy seed forever.

Only after this act of obedience, God spoke to Abram. Until Lot separated from Abram, this covenant that God spoke of between Him and Abram could go no further, because God asked Abram back there in Haran to come out from among them.

I want us all to let this sink deep into our hearts. God said that we are peculiar people; we are a called-out people, a royal priesthood. He has called us out from among them. "Be ye separate," saith the Lord, "be ye not of the world. You're in it but not of it."

God has called us out from the world and sometimes it takes a few trips to Egypt and a few times of humiliation and embarrassment to come out from among them. We are still hanging on to a little bit of disobedience and a little bit of obedience and we are serving two masters. We might have come out of this world, but we brought some of it with us. We brought nephew Lot with us. (Symbolically speaking, we are still hanging on to sin.)

There is a direct connection between power and purity, in obedience and promise; we are talking about the sons of the promise.

Did you know that Abram or his seed has never, ever, totally, occupied land that God gave to him? It has never been or it has never happened!

The Call of Abram

Well, how long is this promise going to affect them?

Forever takes it out of the dimension of time, so when this world has been renovated and renewed, this covenant God makes with us will still be holding or standing. It is forever.

John the Revelator said, "I saw the new heaven and I saw the new earth."

This earth is going to be made new and this promise is still going to be intact, because God said to Abram, "This is for you and your seed forever."

I am not one of the bloodline Jews; nevertheless, I want to tell you what the nation, the descendants of Abraham, are going to posses in the world to come. From the Mediterranean to the Tigress and Euphrates Rivers, and west to the great River of Egypt, the Nile, down to the horns of the Red Sea, up north beyond Dan and Damascus.

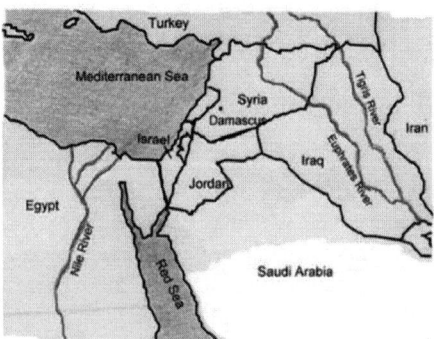

Moreover, it is going to be theirs forever and ever. God cannot lie!

There are promises that God has given you and I that He wants us to take and to have, but there are certain things we need to do to get them. We are studying the Word of God, so we can receive those things that He has promised unto us. There are promises that God has given me that I have not received yet; however, I am after them, but first I have to see them.

All that we see and all that our feet walk over, God will give unto us and ours forever. So if we can see the promises of God as being ours, we can have them. They belong to us and our seed. We're going to have it!

Therefore, I leave you with this....

Acts 2:39 For the promise is unto you and to your children and to all that are afar off, even as many as the Lord our God shall call.

Abram's Alters

Scripture references:
Genesis14:19,20 And he blessed him, and said, "blessed be Abram of the most high God, possessor of heaven and earth: And blessed be the most high God, which hath delivered thine enemies into thy hand. And he gave him tithes of all.

Genesis 12:6,7　　　　Genesis 26:7
Genesis 14:2　　　　　Malachi 3:8-11
Genesis 15:1　　　　　John 4
Genesis 18:1-15　　　 2 Peter 2:22
Genesis 23:2,9,19,20

Our lesson today has many prophetic overtones and symbols. There are three altars and experiences of Abram. Each altar represents a different experience. Then we have Abram's inherited sin; seldom do we find any mark against Abram.

The rescue of Lot and returning from the slaughter. The meeting with Melchizedek and the beginning of the tithe, which is still used as an act of worship today. The purpose of this lesson is to understand the will of God in Abram's life, understand the hour in which he lived, and apply this knowledge to our lives even though we live in a different hour.

In addition, we thank God for this time of study and for this time we have now to lay up treasures in Heaven...

The city of Haran is about 600 miles, northwest from where Terah and Abram started down near the Persian Gulf. They were originally from Ur of the Chaldees, which is right where the Tigress & Euphrates River comes together at the Persian Gulf.

It is about 600 miles from the Persian Gulf to Haran, and then about 300 miles from Haran to Canaan. The reason they went up and down is because of the vast wilderness they had to cross. They are about 900 miles away from where they started, and they traveled with their herds, camels, and so forth.

Altars of God

3 Altars - 3 Experiences

The altars represent instances of obedience. God established it finally in the tabernacle and the temple, that the altar is where man comes on one side and God stands on the other side. This is where man and God come together.

1) <u>Shechem:</u>

Name means "the shoulder."

The Altar of Salvation:

• That first place where Abram pitched his tent in "The Promise Land."
• The Lord appeared unto Abram and he built the first altar unto the Lord in Canaan at Shechem (Genesis 12:7).
• This is the first place that Jacob came back to after he had been 20 years with Laban. He dug a deep well called Jacob's well. The Samaritan woman met Jesus at this well and she received salvation (John 4).

This is a unique and wonderful place; it is a city of refuge. It became a city of refuge to Israel. There are six cities of refuge – three on the east side of Jordan and on the west.

The tribe of Levi had no state because they were the

priestly order, but there were forty-eight (some say fifty-two) cities given to the them. Out of that, six were given as the city of refuge.

These cities of refuge provided sanctuary for people who killed someone accidentally.

Symbolically, there is salvation expressed in our returning or coming back to the promises of God.

2) <u>Bethel:</u>

Name means, "House of God."

• Abram built an altar to the Lord and called upon Him here.
• Jacob stopped on his journey, and there he saw that great ladder with angels ascending and descending.

When Jacob awoke that next morning, he said, "God is in this place." Jacob anointed his pillow, and he and God made a covenant there together. Twenty years after this experience, God changed his name from Jacob to Israel. Therefore, this is a very important place in the history of God's people.

3) <u>Hebron:</u>

Name means "Alliance."

A city of refuge:

• Place where the angels revealed to Abraham that he would have a son (Genesis 18: 1-15).
• Sarah later died at Hebron (Genesis 23:2).

Abraham purchased a parcel of ground in Canaan Land near Hebron. The land had been given unto him, but he had not received his promise yet. Abraham bought a parcel of ground with a cave. He was buried there along with Sarah,

Who Are the Sons of the Promise?

Leah, Rebekah, Isaac, and Jacob. Later, Joseph's bones were brought back to this very place. There is a price we have to pay to die in the promise land, with hope beyond this veil of tears.

• A point of interest: Jacob loved Rachel more than he loved Leah. Leah bore him six sons and Rachel bore him two sons. Lying beside Jacob's bones there at Hebron is not Rachel, but Leah. The messianic line came through Leah and her son Judah.

Rachel was not buried there. Would it surprise you to know that she was buried at Bethlehem?

Rachel is a type and symbol of the suffering Israelites, and her tomb is still of greatly regarded by the Jewish people.

Abram's Inherited Gene?

After Abram came to Bethel and built an altar to God, a drought hit and he went back to Egypt. Abram took with him his beautiful wife, but while he was down there, he made a mistake or sinned. This is really one of the few marks against Abram. Bear in mind that it was against Abram, not Abraham.

What did Abram do in Egypt (type of sin) this time that was so devastating?

While Abram was in Egypt, he knew those men would want his wife, so he said to her, "You tell them you are my sister and they will spare me." Therefore, Sarah told them she was Abram's sister. The Lord visited the king and said, "If you touch that woman, you are a dead man." The king went back, had an embarrassing conversation with Abram, and said, "You have lied to me. This is not your sister, but your wife."

So Abram came back from Egypt like a pup coming

home from a good beating, with his tail between his legs saying, "Man, that was a rough deal."

Abram told this lie, and now something interesting happened later on in history about this.

Are our genes inherited or handed down to the generations?

Sometime later, Isaac lied about Rebekah being his sister (Genesis 26:7).

Isaac told the very same lie his dad had told years before. We need to deal with those weaknesses and conquer them in our lives, so that we do not hand them on to another generation as it was with Lot and Abram.

Lot pitched his tent toward Sodom! All sins come to us in a progressive order.

One doesn't suddenly become a bank robber; he starts by stealing a piece of candy. After Lot pitched his tents toward Sodom, the people came out and said to him, "You are a good man Lot. Come in here and be a judge in our city. Sit here at our gate and judge our people. We need good men like you." However, it cost him everything he had. He lost his daughters and sons-in-laws in the destruction at Sodom and Gomorrah; he lost his wife when she became a pillar of salt.

He would have been better off if the other two daughters had died at Sodom; these two daughters had become the parents of the most wicked people who probably ever walked on the face of God's earth. They came into existence through incest, and it cost Lot his reputation, his family, and everything that was eternal, because he chose for himself. Self is the basis for all sin.

It started back when he made the choice of going to Sodom, the fertile valley and plains. He chose for himself the best. However, Abram made the mistake by bringing

Lot also. When God says, "Come out from among them," that is exactly what He means.

Now comes the Battle of the Kings! Chedorlaomer of Elam, (just east of Babylonia) and three Babylonian kings allied together and took Sodom and Gomorrah as well as some of the sister cities into captivity.

The word of the Lord came to Abram: "Your brother-in-law has been taken captive by the kings of Babylon."

Abram took 318 men, pursued them, and by daybreak, defeated them and sent them running back to Babylon. Abram gathered up all the spoils they had left and headed back home.

The phrase "Abram returning from the slaughter" refers to this battle. When Abram came back, he headed north and down to the regions of the Salt Sea. He stopped at Salem where he met Melchizedek, the king-priest.

This was God's first confirmation that He was going to bring salvation out of Salem.

Salem: Jews rule Salem = Jerusalem!

Melchizedek had neither mother nor father, beginning nor ending of days.

He is symbolizing Christ Himself;

Melchizedek is the only man in the Old Testaments who was both king and priest.

There were many kings and there were many priests, but Melchizedek was a king-priest. Christ is a King-Priest, and His death on Calvary makes Him Lord!

When Abram came to Salem, he was met and blessed by Melchizedek. After he blessed him, Abram gave him a tenth of all that he had. This was a huge offering, because Abram had gold, silver, camels, asses, cattle of all descriptions, and money. He was a very wealthy man.

Of all that Abram had captured from the Babylonian kings, who had made havoc around the entire region, he gave a tenth of it to God. The rest of it he gave back to the kings who lost it.

Genesis 14:23 That I will not take from a thread even to a shoelatchet, and that I will not take anything that is thine, lest thou shouldest say, I have made Abram rich:

Abram would not take so much as a shoelace. However, he gave a tithe (or a tenth) unto Melchizedek and was blessed beyond measure.

Malachi 3: 8-11 Will a man rob God? Yet ye have robbed me. But ye say, Wherein have we robbed thee? In tithes and offerings.Ye are cursed with a curse:for ye have robbed me, even this whole nation. Bring ye all the tithes into storehouse, that there may be meat in mine house and prove me now herewith, saith the Lord of Hosts, if I will not open you the windows of Heaven and pour you out a blessing that there shall not be room enough to receive it.

The principles of tithing began here with the very foundation of salvation, with the King-Priest Melchizedek, the father of Redemption. All of this came together for just a few minutes producing the tithe.

I can tell you personally from my own life that until I learned and was obedient in that area, I was not blessed with the financial blessings of God. I had to come to grip with that reality.

What is the difference in robbing and stealing?

If my neighbor is not home or if he is asleep, and I sneak over and take something, then I have stolen from him. However, if I stick a gun in his face, I am robbing him. I am looking at him, he is looking at me, and I am taking it from him, face to face. God says, "I am standing right here watching you and you are robbing Me. I am looking at you, and you are robbing Me."

Then God says, "Prove Me or test Me!" God has established this principle with Melchizedek and now with Abram.

Abram rescued Lot, met with Melchizedek, and went back home. Poor Lot chose to return to Sodom!

2 Peter 2:22 The dog is turned to his own vomit again; and the sow that was washed to her wallowing in the mire.

What is the Bible saying here?

The wallow is an exterior filth and the vomit is an interior corruption.

We will return to both of them like Lot did if we do not guard against them. God's promises are always hinged on our obedience.

The blessings of Abram start to flow now, but Abram begins to deal with fear.

Genesis 15:1 After these things the word of the Lord came unto Abram in a vision saying, Fear not, Abram: I am thy shield and thy exceeding great reward.

God deals with fear in our lives. Our obedience brings salvation and it will build a hedge of protection around us, sent from God.

God says in His Word, "Now do not be afraid. I will be your shield and I will be your exceeding great reward. There are not enough demons in hell and out of hell to defeat you as long as you are obedient to Me."

Abram says back to God, "How is it, that You are my exceeding great reward when I don't have a son?"

Basically, Abram has the elder servant of his house who is Eliezer of Damascus. He is a son to another, not Abram's son.

Abram is saying here, "What are you going to do to make me productive now? We are well down the scale of time now. I am an old man, and I am pushing 80 sum years old. All I have is Eliezer."

Eliezer of Damascus:

He is symbolic of the Holy Ghost.

Eliezer's name means the same as the Holy Ghost: "God's helper, one along side." He was born unto Abram's servants, inside of the promise land. He was a product of the promise land.

He was born in Damascus, which means "the city of praise."

When do you receive the Holy Ghost?

When you are praising Him, it is a gift. The Holy Ghost is given to us at the city of praise.

Damascus is the city that Saul of Tarsus was not allowed to enter to make havoc for the Christians. God did not allow him to enter the city of praise!

So Abram is saying here, "I have the Holy Ghost, but I want children, a son, a seed."

Symbolically speaking here:

There is a time that Abraham calls in Eliezer and he says, "Eliezer, I have a son Isaac, and I am ready for him to have a bride. I want You, the Holy Ghost, to go back down where I came from and get me a bride for My Son.

Now you cannot take my Son back down there. He has been there once and they crucified Him. He is not going back again until He rides on a white horse and they crown him King of Kings and Lord of Lords. Therefore, Holy Ghost, You have to go down there and get Him a bride." Eliezer went to find Isaac's bride, just like the Holy Ghost was sent to bring the bride back to Christ.

So we now have come into the Promise Land. We have come to the altar at Shechem and got saved.

We have found Eliezer, the Holy Ghost, in our relationship with God. Abram says Eliezer is all he has. God tells Abram, "Come outside and see all the stars in the sky. So shall your seed be."

If you want to be a soul winner, go with Eliezer's help. The promises of God shall be unto you also.

Abram's Sacrifice

Genesis 15:8,9 And he said, Lord, God, whereby shall I know that I shall inherit it? And he said unto him; Take me a heifer of three years old, and a she goat of three years old, and a ram of three years old, and a turtledove and a young pigeon.
Genesis 15: 4,5,6,12,13,14,15,18
Genesis 24:10
Hebrews 5: 8; 13:12-13

One of the more difficult things we have to do in life is stay committed to God. I talk with people today and hear them say, "I am doing things now that I never believed I would." We will water it down if we are not careful. Sometimes we do not stay with our sacrifice.

At any point in his journey with God, if Abram would have backed up or stopped, the journey with God would have been over right there. If he had let the vultures eat that sacrifice, he would not have received the visitation that night. It is better never to make a vow than to break a vow.

Then night came and there was no threat to the sacrifice. There will come a time when people will quit laughing at our Holy Living; the night will come and they will say that person was right. I still contend that the only instrument you and I have to determine love is by sacrifice, the sacrifice that we make, because the rest of it is just words.

Therefore, stay with your sacrifice and keep the blessed promise that God has given us of the Holy Ghost and fire.

God called on Abram to make a commitment and make a sacrifice. God asked him to bring a heifer, goat, ram, and turtle dove and give them as a sacrifice to Him. God has not revealed all there is in this sacrifice He has called on Abram to make.

Red Heifer:

There is discussion about the red heifer and all that is being said in Israel today. This red heifer cannot afford the luxury of having off colored hair. One has been born in the United States and last I heard the Jews have not stamped their approval on this heifer.

Why the Red Heifer?

The red heifer must be sacrificed first, because the red heifer is the purification of the priest. The priest must be purified before he can function in this office. Also, the red heifer must be sacrificed and her ashes scattered without the camp.

Why were her ashes scattered without the camp?

In the New Testament, we learn that Jesus suffered without the gate, (Hebrews 13:12-13) that we might be sanctified. This is purification, the red heifer. So whoever is handling the covenant – mom and dad, preacher, deacon, Sunday school teacher – that is where it begins. It begins with the priest and works it way out through the people. It begins with those who are raising the children and works it way out to the children. It begins with the preacher and works it way out to the congregation. I did not say down, I said out. Therefore, the heifer must be first, because the priest must have righteousness or is in right standing with God.

Goat: I am uncertain whether the goat had to be a she goat, which represents the productivity of those that are going to make the provisions for livelihood.

This goat provides milk, skin for the new wine bottles, hair for clothing, and meat.

Ram: This subject needs more evaluation. The ram symbolizes a headstrong, wanton, or fleshly lust. That ram must be killed; it had to be offered, because of individual wantonness.

Remember Israel, always wanting, causing confusion between God and Israel and Moses. God said to bring Him a ram. There is a way that God can take care of wantonness, and fleshly lust that accompanies us as human entities. The ram must be killed before Abram could receive the inheritance.

Remember that in the ten sons of Jacob, the ram was not dealt with in their lives; their wantonness was such that Jacob could not leave the blessing with them. This ram will be a part of the covenant between God and man. There is more than grace and mercy.

Turtle Dove Pigeon: This was a poor man's sacrifice. The dove or pigeon takes the place of the Paschal Lamb, and incidentally, many of us believe the Paschal Lamb is the blood atonement. The Paschal Lamb itself does not bring blood atonement; it brings us into right standing with God, so we can repent. Abram was called on to make a sacrifice; he placed them on the altar.

He put them in proper order and divided them properly, except the birds, he did not divide. Once Abram made his sacrifice and placed it before God, the vultures came to eat it. Abram drove them away, sustaining and protecting his commitment to God. He would not let his sacrifice be devoured. He would not let it melt away like a bar of soap under a dripping faucet, and he stayed with his sacrifice.

I do not know of a word in the English vocabulary more profanely used than "I love you." The phrase "I cannot hear what you are saying for seeing what you are doing" reflects the importance of being consistent in practicing what we say so we are effective servants for Christ and demonstrate Christ's love.

We must discipline our children to show love. If we fail to do that, we are making a gross mistake. It is unscriptural; we must discipline our children.

Hebrews: 5:8 Though he was a Son, yet learned obedience by the things which he suffered;

Everything that has and will happen to Abram has great prophetic place in our lives today. Abram asked God if Eliezer was going to receive the inheritance. Remember, Eliezer was a symbol of the Holy Ghost. Abram was assured that his seed would receive the inheritance. Abram reminded God that he had no seed.

The work we do for God will affect our seed, our people, and our family and will bring them under God's umbrella. Imagine when Heaven gives out the crowns for soul winning, and you were the Joseph of your household – you were the man that insisted on receiving more from God than just the Holy Ghost. There are many people who receive the Holy Ghost, speak in tongues, and blend in, but that is as far as the Holy Ghost goes in their lives. They never insist on God giving them spiritual children. That is not the inheritance that God had in mind. That is not the will of God for us. He gives us the Holy Ghost so we become His witness; we receive power after the Holy Ghost has come upon us. We will witness in Judea, Jerusalem, and Samaria.

We will witness to people we like and dislike. We will witness to our own and to those half-breed Gentile dogs, those Samaritans! When we have the Holy Ghost, we will be His witness and not our own. It is amazing that we love only who we want when we are commanded to love all God's children.

Abram's Sacrifice

Abram's servant, Eliezer, oversees his household and treasures, just as the Holy Ghost oversees the gifts of the Spirit.

Abram called Eliezer in and said, "Put your hand under my thigh and swear to me that you will not take my son back to my father's people, but you go and bring a bride for my son." Eliezer went and found Rebekah, as the Holy Ghost is finding a bride for Jesus Christ right now.

That is what the Holy Ghost is here for, not to help us blend in and speak in tongues because someone else does. He is here to give us power and find a bride for Jesus Christ.

The bride will be at the well, which is the Spirit of God. She will be willing to water the ten camels, which is the vehicle of the wilderness.

We are laying the foundation for the Holy Ghost in our lives. Before sons were born, the Holy Ghost was in charge, because it is the Spirit that draws. None cometh except those drawn by the Spirit. The Lord assured Abram, "It's not going to end with Eliezer. You will have seed and this land is theirs."

Genesis 15:4,5,6 And behold the word of the Lord came unto him saying, this shall not be thine heir; but he that shall come forth out of thine bowels shall be thine heir. And he brought him forth abroad and said, look now toward heaven and tell the stars, if thou be able to number them: and he said unto him, so shall thy seed be. And he believed in the Lord; and he counted it to him for righteousness.

Genesis 15:12, 13, 14 And when the sun was going down, a deep sleep fell upon Abram; and lo, a horror of great darkness fell upon him. And he said unto Abram, Know of a surety that thy seed shall be a stranger in a land that is not theirs and shall serve them; and they shall afflict those four hundred years; And also that nation, whom they shall serve, will I judge and afterward shall they come out with great substance.

Night came and there was no threat to the sacrifice; the vultures did not come. Once the threat to the sacrifice was over, Abram was faithful in that sacrifice. Now God can talk with Abram, and that is exactly what He did. Remember, three angels had come to the tent of Abram to confirm there would be a child this time next year playing at his tent. Then two of the angels started to Sodom and Gomorrah. One said to the other, "Shall we hide this from Abram?" The other replied, " No, we need not hide it because he will teach his children." So they told Abram they were going to destroy Sodom and Gomorrah if they were wicked. Abram made that great intersession on behalf of Sodom and Gomorrah and those three sister cities. With that in mind, Abram stayed with his sacrifice and God revealed more about the future. Abram would not have had this knowledge had he not stayed with his sacrifice!

God tells Abram his seed will go into another land and be there 400 years. It will not be their land, but when they will come out, they will come with great substance.

What is He saying?

He was telling Abram that his seed would go into Babylonian captivity. When the rulership changed with a new Pharoh, it became a slave situation. Moses instructed the children of Israel before they came out of Egypt: "On the day before Passover, go to all your neighbors and borrow all that you can borrow." They had been slaves without pay and God says, "I am going to pay you, for your work." So all the children of Israel traveled through Egypt asking for gold and silver. God put it on the hearts of the Egyptians to give to them their gold and silver. The Israelites returned home with buckets full of gold and silver.

How do you know this?

When they came out of the wilderness and were ready to build a Tabernacle, Moses said, "Bring me your gold and silver. We are going to build God a Tabernacle." They built gold and silver altars, vessels, lavers, arbors, and gold tables for shew bread. Soon Moses said, "Leave your gold, do not bring any more, we have too much." Remember God said, "When they come out I am going to pay them with great substance." We are going to be paid for what we do for God also.

Genesis 15:15 And thou shalt go to thy fathers in peace; thou shalt be buried in a good old age.

Abram and Sarah were very bewildered that they could have children when Sarah was 90 and Abram was 100 years old. When God touched that 100-year-old man, he married another woman after Sarah died and had six more boys and who knows how many girls. God told them, "I am going to do it for you!" And He did. God can do the impossible!

Genesis 15:18 In the same day the Lord made a covenant with Abram saying, unto thy seed have I given this land, from the river of Egypt unto the great river, the river Euphrates:

To this day, the promise that God gave Abram concerning the land has never been totally and completely fulfilled. God has given unto Abram and his seed after him the land that actually begins at the cradle of the human race.

Who Are the Sons of the Promise?

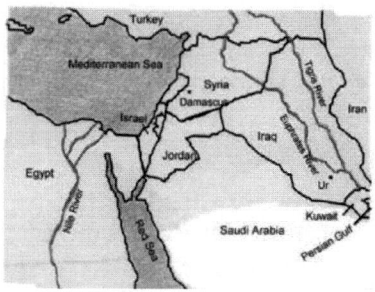

The land God is going to give Abram's seed includes the land from the Tigress and Euphrates Rivers around Kuwait (Ur of the Chaldees) to the Red Sea, and from the horns of the Red Sea to the River Nile and up beyond Damascus. They obtained a portion of this, but have never fully received the promise of God. It will happen and there will be a day, maybe in the world to come, that the full promise of God will belong to those to whom He promised. I want to encourage you children that the full promise of God will come to you. We have accepted Christ, the Anointed One, the Messiah, and we are the Gentiles. When the Tabernacle was pitched in the wilderness, on the west end of the camp was the Tribe of Ephraim, Manasseh, and Benjamin. The Tabernacle had four sides and there were twelve tribes, so on each side there were three tribes. When they stopped, they put up the Tabernacle, everyone was in the right order, or everyone was right where they belonged. Naturally, on the east is Judah, toward the rising of the sun. On the west are the Gentiles, Ephraim, Manasseh, and Benjamin, with Benjamin being the last son, consequently the only son born in the promise land.

Ephraim and Manasseh were sons by Joseph and his Egyptian wife, so they were from a Gentile woman. They represent the order of the Gentiles. God is our Father (type of Joseph), the Church is our mother and she is Gentile. Benjamin is the only son of the twelve born in the promise land representing the Christian today who is born in the promise land (saved by the promises of God).

When they were moving north, everything marched

in that order. When they were moving from the Red Sea, they came up and started out east a little ways. Judah was leading it. When they went north, those on the north tribe led it, but when they moved towards the desert and were headed to the promise land, Benjamin led.

The Gentiles today are leading the way into the promises of God, into the promise land and the Jews will be the last to accept Christ as their Savior and will be the last one in as a nation.

When it was time to go into the promise land the Gentiles must lead – that is you and me. We have the promise land.

When Jesus introduces the Gentile Bride standing above that Wailing Wall in Jerusalem at the close of Tribulations we are going to be there. We will be leading it!

I am going to be following a man on a white steed and every time he turns around, he will bump into me!

You see, I am one of those Gentile dogs that God loves. He put us in the forefront and when He lands on that Mount of Olives, I will be there. When he crosses Kidron Valley, I will be there; when He comes through the great Eastern Gate, I will be there.

When we stand and look down from that Wailing Wall, that nation is weeping because of the blood bath of Armageddon. Jesus Christ will say, "Here is my bride." And I will be there.

Abram & The Church

Scripture reference:
Genesis 16: 3,5,6 And Sarai, Abram's wife, took Hagar her maid the Egyptian, after Abram had dwelt ten years in the land of Canaan, and gave her to her husband Abram to be his wife. (These verses 5 & 6 in part) And Sarai said unto Abram, My wrong be upon thee: But Abram said unto Sarai, behold thy maid is in thy hand;
Genesis 16:1,2,4,5,6,7,9,10,11,12
Matthew 24:24; 26:41
Romans 14:5

Abram was living as we live and God has potential right in us, where we live. There are several steps that we have to make, to reach our full potential. It is progressive, as we grow in the grace and knowledge of the Lord. Abram has been making several steps, as he moves toward his potential in the kingdom of God and to find his place in eternity and to find his place on earth. Who has had a greater affect among earthen vessels? What human being has greatly affected the human race than Abraham?

We are looking to the schoolmaster that is in Abraham, to teach us those things that will assist us in our contribution here on earth and our state in the world to come. I do not know of anyone in the Old Testament that has had a greater impact and greater influence on the human race than Abraham has. That is the reason he has become the schoolmaster that he is.

We are studying Abraham's life, so that we can learn how to be the Sons of the Promise, the true sons.

Genesis chapter 16 is a fundamental foundation that

we must understand especially in this hour of deception. I call your attention to Jesus teaching the disciples on their way to Calvary. He taught them repeatedly to pray so they would not be tempted.

Matthew 26:41 Watch and pray that ye not enter into temptation: the spirit indeed is willing, but the flesh is weak.

Today, He repeatedly teaches that we should pray and not be deceived. Not deception regarding who the true Son is, but deception in what true Salvation is. We need to understand some details that have led the world into the deception we are in today.

Matthew 24:24 For there shall arise false Christs and false prophets and shall show great signs and wonders; insomuch that, if it were possible, they shall deceive the very elect.

There are many ways that the leering lights of this world deceive us. The devil will try to deceive us through any way he can - finances, religion, etc. However, if there is no way for us to be deceived then we will not be. It is that simple. Therefore, we will study the next step that Abram is making to move toward that 100-fold in the kingdom of God. The Bible teaches us that there are 30-60-90-100-fold Christians. We start out in that first act of obedience, which is salvation. We could stay there, and in the world to come, we will be servants. We take the next step, which is sanctification. Next is obedience and commitment and God's assistance through the Holy Ghost. As we go up the realm we become a blessing to everyone. This is the realm of God's economy and this is how He is moving.

The Church, Sarah, will have a baby and he will be the Ephesians 4 child. He will be in the fullness of Jesus Christ. She is going to have a son, but she has not responded as we wanted her to. The Church is going to produce a Bride

Who Are the Sons of the Promise?

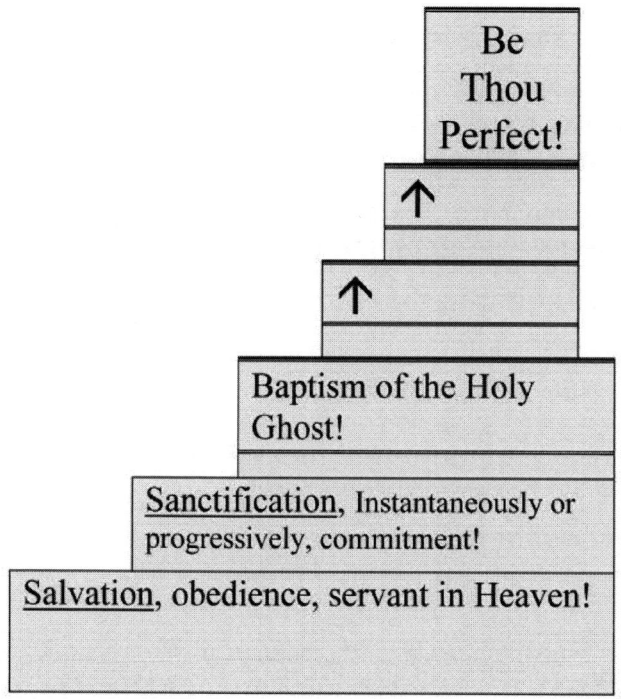

Hood Order, and I am determined to be a part of it. Our faith has grown weak. The Church world has stepped into this situation and has begun to make some detrimental compromises that only God will be able to turn around.

Genesis 16: 1,2,3 Now Sarah, Abram's wife bare him no children: and she had a handmaid an Egyptian, whose name was Hagar. And Sarah said unto Abram, Behold now the Lord hath restrained me from bearing: I pray thee go in unto my maid; it may be that I may obtain children by her. And Abram hearkened to the voice of Sarah. And Sarah, Abram's wife, took Hagar her maid the Egyptian, after Abram had dwelt ten years in the land of Canaan and gave her to her husband Abram to be his wife.

Hagar was brought in by Sarah and Sarah gave Hagar to Abram; it was not Abram who received Hagar.

Sarah represents the Church. The Church gave Abram the half-breed.

We need to know where all the worldliness, which we are hanging onto in the Church, came from. Let every man be fully persuaded in his own mind (Romans 14:5).

More happened in that hour than we are able to understand. In addition, much has happened in the fulfillment of the Church age, beginning in the 60s and progressing through the 70s and 80s.

Let us begin to put things in order: Abram, Sarai, Hagar, and ten years in the promise land.

What does the number ten mean?

Completion.

By the time they had been there ten years, their values should have been established. Abram is now 86 years old. If he was going to have a son, with Sarai, his wife, it should have already happened. She became impatient with God's timing. Even though Sarah had the promise of a son, she took matters into her own hands and she gave Hagar, the Egyptian, to Abram to be his wife.

We can compare Sarai giving Hagar to Abraham with the Church today. The church has reached out and embraced the sins of the world. We can't build a Church numerically the way we want to build it, so we have let the world in to help us! We reached out as a Church and embraced the world to get a son for numbers.

Here is a sad commentary: Abram would not have had Hagar, the Egyptian, if Sarah had not given Hagar to Abram.

Who Are the Sons of the Promise?

That single act brought consequences into this world – never a time of peace or possession. This is the foundation of the war that will last until the war of Armageddon. The battle in Israel and around the world today is because of Hagar and Ishmael.

When Abram accepted Hagar as his concubine wife, God did not speak to him for thirteen years. Abram made another mistake. God told Abram to come out from his kindred at Haran, but he brought Lot. It caused Abram a lot of grief and trouble, and it cost Lot everything he had. When Abram lied to Pharaoh about Sarai, it caused Abram a lot of embarrassment and self-respect. But thank God, He is a God of another chance and He still forgives.

Do you understand what I am saying? How can that be?

Therefore, we as the Church have invited Hagar in and we have produced some half-breeds: half Christian and half worldly.

Genesis 16:4,5 And he went in unto Hagar, and she conceived; and when she saw that she had conceived, her mistress was despised in her eyes. And Sari said unto Abram, My wrong be upon thee: I have given my maid into thy bosom; and when she saw that she had conceived, I was despised in her eyes: the Lord judge between me and thee.

When Sarah saw that Hagar had conceived, she rose up against this and said, "I made a mistake and started pressuring Hagar." Sarah then makes a second mistake and blames Abram. That sounds like dialogue coming straight from the Garden of Eden. It is amazing that we cannot judge ourselves in areas that need our undivided attention. When Sarah saw that Hagar conceived and when Hagar saw that she had conceived, Hagar became egotistical and Sarah began blaming Abram, because he was the one having a child by the Egyptian. When the Lord came to Adam and asked, "What have you done?" Adam said, "It's the woman you gave me." When the Lord went to Eve, Eve blamed the serpent. It is amazing that we cannot just look at life and say, "This is what I have done. God, I need some help with it." It would have been wonderful if Adam had taken Eve by the hand that evening when he came in and found that she had eaten of the tree, and said, "Honey, we need to go to the gate. He will be here in a little bit and we are going to ask for some help. We have a problem."

Instead, we blame it on someone else, right? Sarah sees that she has made a mistake, and I do not believe she had a clue how big the mistake was. Nevertheless, she said, "This mistake is your fault." Abram replies, "Do whatever you want to do." His response left it in their sovereignty, their choices. Instead of Sarah returning or replying with a Christian attitude, she becomes very embittered and very hostile toward Hagar and Hagar fled. Hagar leaves Abram's tent twice, once before Ishmael is born and once after.

Genesis 16: 6,7,9 But Abram said unto Sarai, Behold thy maid is in thy hand; do to her as it pleaseth thee. And when Sari dealt harshly with her, she fled from her face. And the angel of the Lord found her by the fountain of water in the wilderness, by the fountain in the way of Shur. And the angels of the Lord said unto her, Return to thy mistress and submit thyself under her hands.

Now, this particular time, she left Abram's tent and headed back to Egypt. The Angel of the Lord met her at the well and says, "Hagar, you have conceived; you are the mistress to Sarah." The angel gave her no slack. He said, "You are Sarah's mistress; return to your post of duty." God always has a chain of command, and will never break that chain of command. He will never get out of step. That is one of the promises we were given in the new covenant. No man will get out of step and we will stay in our position. Sarah may be making some mistakes, but that does not justify Hagar making one.

Genesis 16:10,11,12 And the angel of the Lord said unto her. I will multiply thy seed exceedingly, that it shall not be numbered for multitude. And the angel of the Lord said unto her, Behold thou art with child, and shalt bear a son and shalt call his name Ishmael; because the Lord hath heard thy affliction. And he will be a wild man; his hand will be against everyman and everyman's hand against him; and he shall dwell in the presence of all his brethren.

Later the Lord tells us that Ishmael will be like an Arabian ass, which cannot be bridled. This has plagued your life and my life and the Church, down through the ages. Some of us will get out of position and out of step, from the position where God placed us and we will take the bits. Those of you that ride horses know that when we say a horse takes his bits, he pays no attention, you can't guide him anywhere. The origin of the donkey's name is from the Arabian ass. They are bull headed, hardheaded, rebellious, and stubborn just like the Arabian ass. That mule is going to do what he wants to do, short of killing himself. The angel of the Lord is saying to Hagar, "Your son is going to be out of control. No one will control him, and he will take his bits." It does not matter whether Ishmael as the elder, will ever able to recognize that Isaac is the promise child. He will send his entire legion to hell, before he will ever recognize that Sarah's son is the true son.

What would cause me to stand up and say, "It is my way or the highway?"

Ishmael represents rebellion, the attitude that says, "My way or the highway." This is the spirit that would cause me to stand up and say, "This is the way it will happen." It is the spirit of a half- breed. Being half-Christian and half-world, we must judge our own heart.

Joseph married an Egyptian woman and had two sons. Why wasn't Joseph's wife considered a half-breed?

Egyptian Hagar was not a true follower of the God of Israel. She was a hand servant, and she never became a love servant. She was angry with Sarah and it consumed her.

Now on the other hand, Joseph's Egyptian wife wanted to be a servant to the God that Joseph served. She wanted to walk in love whereas Hagar did not. Her heart was not right. We need to ask ourselves these questions:

- Is my heart right with God?

- Do I walk in love?

- Do I have a servant's heart?

- Am I willing and obedient, or am I rebellious?

We need to judge these things in our lives if we want to be a part of the Bride Hood order!

Abram-Abraham

Scripture references:
Genesis 17:1,4,24 I am almighty God; walk before me and be thou perfect. (In-part) Neither shall thy name anymore be called Abram, but thy name shall be Abraham; for a father of many nations have I made thee. And Abraham was ninety years old and nine, when he was circumcised in the flesh of his foreskin.

Genesis 17:2,3,5,6,8,9,10,14,18	Phil. 3:3
Matthew 4:16	Col. 2:11
Luke 12:47-48	Hebrews 13:12
Romans 2:28-29; 7:19,21; 5:8	Revelations 12:10

We are endeavoring to study the 17th chapter of the book of Genesis. I want you to understand that there is so much in the life of Abraham, but you will notice that this is true with Moses and with David and with all good men and women of the Bible, in the areas that God has ordained. One thing I think is so noteworthy is the fact that this is true in our lives, when we find ourselves in obedience to God. Everything that Abraham was to his lineage, you and I are to ours. Everything that he was to his people, you and I are to our people.

Jesus Christ has given us greater promises and a better covenant. In addition, this covenant is going to do a greater work even in our lives than that which happened to those in the lineage of Abraham. We will spend time in chapter 17 as we learn of our lives today and reach into our eternities in a greater dimension and in a greater means. Abram is now about to take another step up the ladder.

Genesis 17:1 And when Abram was ninety years old and

nine, the Lord appeared to Abram, and said unto him, I am the Almighty God; walk before me, and be thou perfect.

Abram is ninety-nine years old when the Lord appears unto him this time. Ishmael was born unto Abram when he was about 85 years old. Previously God appeared to him and said," I am your shield and I am your exceeding great reward." This tells us how God will be dealing with conversation between Him and Abram. He comes to him when he is 99 years old and says, "I am the Lord, the Almighty God; I am going to do something that is supernatural. I am from before the beginning, the omnipresent God, and I am capable of doing anything that I choose to do."   Not only is He the Almighty God, but He said, "Walk before Me and be thou perfect." God uses the word perfect, and it is used differently in different versions of the Bible. Here are a few:

- King James Version: Perfect

- Modern language: Upright

- Living Bible: Obedience

- Revised Standard: Blameless

Look at what is held within the framework of perfection. That word perfection does strange things to our mentality when we just take it in. The word perfect is a big word!

Like the word predestination, it gets out of hand and gets into some areas that maybe God is not intending it to reach. God wants us to be perfect and we want to talk about that. We think of perfection as reaching a realm wherein we are totally in the likeness of God as Ephesians 4 says. In essence this means walk before Him in perfect obedience and understand that we have limitations. God understands that life experiences, our birthplace, our family, and many other factors shape each of us. He is not expecting total perfection as we think of total perfection. With all of our hearts we want to be an obedient person. The word walk refers to our everyday life. God says, "Walk thou before Me. Walk before Me and be thou perfect." What is perfection for one person is not perfection for another person. God's standards are all the same.

How can that be if God is no respecter of persons?

Because of our limitations, our relationship, our maturity, etc, our perfection levels are different. Expectations of a newborn baby are different than a grown man and woman. A soldier sent overseas to do battle has a different perfection and a different maturity. The enemy likes to accuse us in our Christian walk.

Revelation 12:10 And I heard a loud voice saying in Heaven, Now Is come salvation and strength and the Kingdom of our God And the power of his Christ: For the accuser of our brethren is cast down, which accused them before our God day and night.

Personal reference:

I used to tell my boys when they were younger and at home, "What God has given you and required of you is going to be totally different than anyone else sitting in your classroom. You may be going to school with three hundred seniors and there is not another senior in that class that has the knowledge and the understanding of the Word of God that you have. Their perfection is different from your perfection. Where much is given, much is required."

Luke 12:47,48 But he that knew not and did commit things worthy of stripes shall be beaten with few stripes, For unto whomsoever much is given, of him shall be much required: and to whom men have committed much, of him they will ask more.

Abram is about to take another step up the ladder in becoming all that he can become. God wants obedience: "Be thou perfect. I am the Almighty God and I am now ready to make an additional, more complete covenant with you." We need to take all limitations off Him and let us understand that He can do anything, He is Almighty!

The Bible instructs us to extend our tent stakes and enlarge our borders. We are going to reach out further now!

Genesis 17:2 And I will make my covenant between me and thee, and will multiply thee exceedingly.

We have talked about obedience, salvation, and mistakes with Abram.

Now we will discuss perfection and slipping more into the eternal aspect, reaching beyond the earthly things and into the heavenly things.

Abram has proven himself to God. The Covenant is between him and God, and it will affect millions. You, Abram will have a personal eternity as each of us will. Our personal eternity, our life, our walk, and our perfection here will effect eternity.

Genesis 17:3,4 And Abram fell on his face: and God talked to him saying, As for me, behold my covenant is with thee, and thou shalt be a father of many nations.

God has not revealed Abraham's part of the covenant, but does reveal what he will do for Abram. This is where things go from Abram to the masses. In Revelation 2 and 3, God addresses the seven Churches of Asia, telling them what was good and what He appreciated and admired in them. Then to five of the churches, "I have something against you." He then told them the things they needed to do. He addressed Abram in the same manner: "I have a covenant a goal, a dream, a desire. Your potential is to be the father of nations and bless multitudes. Your name is going to be great; you will be wealthy and famous."

Sadly, today Abraham has more followers than Jesus Christ. That is not Abraham's fault.

Now how can that be?

Abraham is recognized by the Jewish, Christian, and Islam religions, but only Christians follow Jesus Christ. Abraham has more followers, but he did not give his life for them to be saved. They are lost; there is only one name given among men where by we shall be saved and that is Jesus Christ.

Genesis 17:5 Neither shall thy name any more be called Abram, but thy name shall be Abraham; for a father of many nations have I made thee.

The name Abram means "father of elevation." He is exalted, elevated, and a leader. The name Abraham means "father of a multitude." The covenant with God puts him in a different realm, and so his name changes. Earlier in the Bible he was called Abraham, but he was never Abraham until he made this covenant. This is a direct covenant that you and I find in our lives that changes our name. God changed everyone's name in the Bible that dedicated their lives to Him. Sometimes a king would change the name.

Whose name was first changed in the Bible that we know about?

Lucifer!

He lost his relationship, his name was Lucifer, and he lost that name. He was an archangel, created as an angel of light or bearer of light, but now, his name is Satan, which means adversary.

Abram is now Abraham and Sarai is Sarah. Saul was changed to Paul. A name change in those days expressed one's calling, purpose, and fulfillment in life.

Genesis 17:6 And I will make thee exceeding fruitful, and I will make nations of thee, and kings shall come out of thee.

After Sarah's death, Abraham married another woman. She bore him six sons, and they became fathers of nations. We understand what God is going to do through Abraham. You and I also have a covenant with God through the blood of Jesus Christ. God wants to do a great work, so the covenant came into existence before the son of promise was born. Isaac had not yet been born, but the promise is there. There are things in our lives that God has promised. Hold on to God's hand, and He will fulfill His promises.

Genesis 17:8,9 And I will give unto thee and to thy seed after thee, the land wherein thou art a stranger, all the land of Canaan, for an everlasting possession; and I will be their God. And God said unto Abraham, Thou shalt keep my covenant therefore, thou, and thy seed after thee in their generations.

This scripture takes it out of the dimension of time. This is an everlasting covenant, forever and ever.

On the new earth that John saw in his revelation, Israel, then and only then, will for the first time possess all the land that God promised Abraham.

The promise that God made Abraham was land from the Red Sea to the horns, Sinai, west to the Nile, over to the Tigress Euphrates Valley on the East. The Jews have never possessed all that, because God has made this

Who Are the Sons of the Promise?

an everlasting covenant. In the new world, the nation of Israel will occupy this area. Remember John said that he saw a new heaven, a new earth, and the seas were no more. The nation of Israel as a whole has many promises awaiting them. This earth will be ruled out of Jerusalem, throughout the ceaseless ages of eternity and during the Millennium age also.

However, the thing that I want you to see is that because these Jews have rejected Christ, their promises are earthly. They can receive heavenly promises along with us individually, but as a nation, they will never turn to Christ until the close of the Battle of Armageddon.

The Abrahamic covenant is an everlasting promise. As long as we are tempted and living as we live today, Abraham's part of the covenant will still be binding. Verse ten describes Abraham's part of the covenant.

Genesis 17:10,14 This is my covenant, which ye shall keep, between me and you and thy seed after thee; every man child among you shall be circumcised. And ye shall circumcise the flesh of your foreskin; and it shall be a token of the covenant betwixt me and you. And he that is eight days old shall be circumcised among you, every man-child in your generations, he that is born in the house or bought with money of any stranger, which is not of thy seed. He that is born in thy house and he that is bought with thy money, must be circumcised; and my covenant shall be in you flesh for an everlasting covenant. And the uncircumcised man-child whose flesh of his foreskin is not circumcised, that soul shall be cut off from his people; he hath broken my covenant.

Incidentally, Moslems keep the covenant of circumcision. Ishmael was thirteen years old when Abraham kept the covenant of circumcision.

In the covenant with Isaac and the Jews, circumcision took place on the eighth day after birth. When Jesus was eight days old, He was brought to the temple and Simeon and Anna received Him.

What is the covenant in our day regarding circumcision?

Reference: Romans 2:28-29

Romans 15:8

Philippians 3:3

The apostle explains circumcision is the flesh but Jesus is going to bring us to circumcision inwardly, or the circumcision of the heart, through the spirit. In the Old Testament, the word circumcision refers to sanctification in the New Testament.

Sanctification in the New Testament is circumcision in the Old Testament.

Hebrews 13:12 Wherefore Jesus also, that he might sanctify the people, with his own blood, suffered without the gate.

This is beautiful. He brought us the experience of sanctification, which is purifying or cleansing. This happens when the axe is put to the root of the tree.

Remember John the Baptist made the statement: "When He comes He will thoroughly purge his floor." He is referring to the threshing floor. Stocks of wheat are thrown on the floor and tromped on. They break and the stock is sorted from the grain, but the grain still has a membrane over it called the chaff. Next, the corn of wheat is walked on until the membrane breaks loose. Then it is placed on a great threshing floor, which might be fifteen to eighteen feet in diameter with a wall about four foot high.

Who Are the Sons of the Promise?

A fan is pulled through the threshing floor and the wind from the fan picks up the chaff, and whips it up in the air and out of the threshing floor.

Our soul is a fleshly membrane and that membrane must be sanctified.

Romans 15:8 Now I say that Jesus Christ was a minister of the circumcision for the truth of God, to confirm the promises made unto the fathers.

This scripture refers to the promises that come to us through the cleansing and the sanctification that Jesus Christ brought us, through the Spirit of God in the cleansing of this earthen vessel, and bringing our flesh in subjection to the will of God. He said He would put the axe to the root of the tree. An Elm tree can be cut down but the root system is still there. When we ask for God's forgiveness, we are forgiven. The tree is gone, but the thing that caused it is still there. Putting the axe to the root of the tree kills the tree and the root system. This is what sanctification does. It takes the damnable nature and brings it into subjection to the will of God. It does not make us robots; we have the power of choice. It simply breaks the chain. There are chains that are fleshly, physical, mental, and genetic. We can choose not to give in to genetic predispositions with the help of the Lord, thus, breaking the genetic cycle. Sometimes we have an inherited gene that has not been dealt with. It can be passed from father to son and mother to daughter, and it keeps being handed down the lineage. God wants to put the axe to the root of that tree. The same thing that destroyed Grandma, I saw in my mother. What destroyed my mother's perfection can destroy mine. I need the Lord to put an axe to the damnable nature in my life. Some people are relaxed and are pleasant to be around or easy to work with. There are others that strike or get offended. Some folks you cannot talk freely with because they can become angry quickly, twist words, are defensive, and unapproachable.

Anyone should be able to come to us, and speak about anything, and not be worried we will be offended or upset. This covenant of circumcision is for us. Then we need to be sanctified.

Why do so many people think that sanctification is just outward appearance?

I would have to say that each of us is unique. Opinions are like eternities, everyone has one. That is no sign that it is good and right. Yesteryear, I think we spent more time preaching and teaching on the visible sense of sanctification. Somehow, we did not deal much with the inward experience of sanctification. Why do we do that?

I cannot answer that because we are all unique. How you perceive some things and how someone else perceives some things are very different. Depending on their depth and their ability, there are certain subjects that none of us deal with. We only preach and teach on subjects or experiences that we have had. I will never teach on how to be a mother. I will never be one, so I do not know how to be a mother.

I leave you with this thought. We can only preach and teach about experiences that we know or experiences that we have been through. We teach where are.

Abraham & Predestination

Scripture references:
Genesis 17:10,18, 16:12 This is my covenant, which ye shalt keep my covenant therefore, thou, and thy seed after thee in their generations. And Abraham said unto God, O that Ishmael might live before thee! And he will be a wild man; his hand will be against every man and every man's hand against him; and he shall dwell in the presence of all his brethren.

Matthew 4:16	Galatians 6: 7,8
Luke 12:47,48	Colossians 2:11
Romans 7:19,21,24	Hebrews 13:12

Genesis 17 is a wonderful study. The fathers of twilight were only serving through a flicker of light.

Yet their lives lined up with a scenario that is revealed to us today. I cannot see anything but the direct hand of God in their lives bringing them to the position where they so accurately and adequately fulfilled prophecy. Their lives gave us a clearer understanding today of what Gods plan is for our lives. We are dealing with the third step in Abraham's journey through life. He is on the third realm. Each realm brings him into a greater blessing, but with greater acts of obedience. God leaves us the power to choose, and the consequence of those choices can reach out unto the third and fourth generations.

It is very important that we understand that no man lives to himself and no man dies to himself. The choices that have been made are affecting our lives today will affect our lives tomorrow

<u>Scripture reference for Predestination:</u>

Romans 8:29   Ephesians 1:5,11   2 Timothy 2:19

The Lord called Abram to be perfect, to walk upright with integrity before Him. There is a difference in lifestyle between a saint who is serving God with total integrity and a man or woman who is casually, occasionally, and half-hazardly serving the Lord. When looking into the lives of those that lived before us, those that touched our lives, we see their integrity or their lack of integrity.

Galatians 6:7,8 Be not deceived; God is not mocked: for whatsoever a man soweth, that shall he also reap. For he that soweth to his flesh shall of the flesh reap corruption; but he that soweth to the Spirit shall of the Spirit reap life everlasting.

If you sow good seed, then you will have a good harvest. If you sow bad seed then you will have a bad harvest. This is God's law of sowing and reaping. Perfection enlarges our boundaries, and perfection in this hour is like a light in the night that can be seen from afar. However, if the light is not there you are groping in the darkness like every one else.

While we were working in Africa, we were driving home after late services one night. We were on the old cow trail trying to get to a better road, and we passed hundreds of people walking at night. We saw them at 11:00 or 12:00 at night or 2:00 in the morning. We passed them going 40 miles per hour; they were just standing there in the night. I wondered how they could see. Where were they going? Why were they out this time of night? As we drove down the road in the middle of the night, they looked like fence post when we passed them. This was bewildering to me. There was no light; it was complete darkness.

When you and I walk in the light, people see us and

are drawn to us, but when we grope in darkness, we are just beaten men walking beaten paths. That is why Jesus said:

Matthew 4:16 The people whom sat in darkness saw great light; and to them which sat in the region and shadow of death light is sprung up.

Well, you can imagine those African people out there at midnight, walking home in pitch darkness, when suddenly comes a single light from the vehicle we were in. They would just stand there and watch the light go by. It was amazing!

Abraham had been called into perfection and that is a greater light.

In the Book of Revelation, you will find that there are letters to the Seven Churches of Asia. Starting with the church at Ephesus and ending with the church at Laodicea, God requires more of the next Church, and He gives greater reward to that Church. In other words, where much is given, much is required.

Luke 12:47-48 And that servant which knew his Lord's will and prepared not himself; neither did according to his will, shall be beaten with many stripes. But he that knew not and did commit things worthy of stripes shall be beaten with few stripes. For unto whomsoever much is given, of him shall be much required: and to whom men have committed much, of him they will ask the more.

More is required of us when we have more light. There are degrees in hell and degrees in eternal life with God. Now more is required of Abraham because his relationship with God is superior to anyone around him. His knowledge of God surpasses everyone around him. God declared, "Be thou perfect. Your name is no longer Abram but Abraham, and your wife's name is no longer Sarai but Sarah." That changed her from being "my princess"; she is becoming "a princess." She is mother to nations now. She is not just Abraham's wife, and she will affect unborn generations, since this event has taken place. She in essence is the Church and belongs to everyone. God told Abraham about how he would be blessed, and now God speaks about the covenant of circumcision.

(See Romans 7-8 chapter for further study.)

Romans 7:19,21,24 For the good that I would I do not: but the evil which I would not, that I do. I find then a law, that, when I would do good, evil is present with me. O wretched man that I am! Who shall deliver me from the body of this death?

Now all of us have seen that member in our body, have we not? That is the lower nature of man. In the Book of Genesis, God breathed the breath of life into Adam's nostrils – a form, a fleshly body, not a hunk of clay. That separated us from the animal kingdom even though we were both created on the sixth day. We became a living soul, we were breath out of God and we were breath out of eternity, God's eternity. We will return to eternity; we will always be and will never cease to be. Your body may lie down for a season in the grave, but it will come back, and your soul will be reunited with it and the mortal will take on immortality, corruption will become incorruptible. We were breathed out of eternity by God, so we will return to eternity. He was breathing into the fleshly body.

This leads us to the subject of the covenant of circumcision. The flesh must be circumcised, therefore, every male must be circumcised.

Hebrews 13:12 Wherefore Jesus also, that he might sanctify the people with his own blood, suffered without the gate.

Who Are the Sons of the Promise?

Colossians 2:11 In whom also ye are circumcised with the circumcision made without hands, in putting off the body of the sins of the flesh by the circumcision of Christ:

Christ sanctifies us. The trouble we have in this world is trouble with the flesh. That is why, when they crucified our Lord and Savior, they did not crucify His spirit or soul, but they crucified the flesh. We are weak in the flesh. They put a crown of thorns on his flesh, drove nails in the flesh, and pierced the flesh. Flesh is our source of sin. If we followed our spirit or soul after being born again, all our desires would be good and right. We would go to heaven and be reunited with our father. However, we live in earthly vessels and we still have battles with the flesh. If we did not have that battle, we would not be rewarded eternally, We are created free mortal agents. We must make the choice to serve our Lord. If we were perfect, we could not be rewarded.

In your garden where you live, there is a tree of good and evil. It must be there, we cannot build a moral character without it. The eternal world is based on what we did with that tree of good and evil while we are here, but that is in eternity and we are not there yet. We still live in earthly vessels and must be crucified, or the flesh will dominate our life and destroy our eternity.

The covenant is about crucifying the flesh, which is demonstrated through circumcision.

There is no substitute for self-discipline. We choose to do it or not. It is up to us and this is our sovereignty; consequences will follow. Until we receive dying grace, we will have flesh to contend with. The battlefield is holiness, the battle cry is evangelism, and we are in that place now.

Abraham has come to the place where he is ready to contend with the flesh. Abraham is promised a son by

Sarah, Sarah is going to have a baby; the Church is going to have a man-child. It does not matter whether I'm in it or not; it is going to happen. There will be an order of perfected saints. Not perfect in people eyes, you cannot please people. Too many of us often have Satan near us and he is the accuser of the brethren. So whatever room we make in our lives for the adversary that part of us is going to be judging and condemning people who are trying to live perfect. In other words, if I am a thirty-fold Christian, 70% of me will be critical of others.

How much room I leave in my life for the devil is how critical and self-centered I am. When God created man and put him in the garden, he was God-centered. As he was tilling, watching, gardening, he was worshiping, walking, and talking daily with God. He was God-centered.

Then man chose to serve another, and from that day until this day, man has been self-centered, and that is sin. God telling Abraham that he would have a son by Sarah was incomprehensible.

Like the new birth, it is a miracle, only through Christ.

Sarah and Hagar are the two women in Abraham's life at this time.

• Hagar, is the Egyptian. Egypt represents a type of sin.

• Sarah represents the Church.

• Hagar could conceive from Abram but could not conceive from Abraham!

• Sarah could conceive from Abraham but could not conceive from Abram!

Abram was "a father," but Abraham is "the father of a multitude." He is the father of the promised son and the

Who Are the Sons of the Promise?

promised seed.

Abraham became the father of Isaac, the promised man with the promised son! Abram was learning obedience, sin conceived of him, and here came Ishmael. Therefore, when you and I live in perfection, this world will not be able to conceive of us, even when we are striving for perfection. Abraham found Sarah, the mother of the promised son. This world will never produce the sons of the promise, but the Church will produce the sons of the promise! If our sons and daughters have any future in the world to come, it will be through the Church.

We started this lesson discussing the sons of the promise. All the sons of the promise come through the Church, and not one of them will ever come through Hagar or through the world.

I know we went off and played in the world and this is the reason we have problems with Sarah conceiving from us. If we are earthly minded, casual, disobedient children of God, giving God a little portion of our lives while giving the devil a larger portion of our lives, then we need not expect our children to be sons of the promise.

We can try to prop it up on seven sides trying to make it stand, but I want you to know that the Church is the one who is going to have Isaac, the man-child. We need not expect our children to go any further than our integrity and dedication to God.

Genesis 17:18 And Abraham said unto God, O that Ishmael might live before thee.

Abraham was pleading with God about Ishmael. However, God has told him this...

Genesis 16:12 Ishmael will be a wild man; his hand against every man and every man against him; and he shall dwell in the presence of all his brethren.

While Abraham was pleading with God about Ishmael, we see the heart of a father and the heart of a preacher, and I see the heart of those that are pleading today. The greatest picture of this statement will be during the tribulations and at the White Throne Judgment. In addition, for those who have been disobedient, the rapture itself is a form of judgment. Those who are ready will go, while those who are not ready will stay. That is a judgment. God judges those who are not ready to go and they stay. But when we get to that great judgment scene and God says, "Depart from Me you disobedient," I will say, "Now wait a minute God, what about my son?"

Abraham pleaded with God about Ishmael, but Ishmael refused to be bridled. There was nothing Abraham could do about his disobedience. The power of choice is ours; it does not matter what we have purposed to do for God, nor how the devil fights us. If we choose to do the will of God, God will make a way where there seems to be no way. God will help us do exactly what we want to do for Him. He will make a way for us in this world and the world to come, and it will happen through the Church.

We are only a part of the Church of God, and God is going to have a son of obedience.

As we follow Isaac, he is a man liken unto God. We have heard very little about this man-child and how he spent his life in submission and peace. When we look into the life of Abraham, the covenant, and the covenant sons, we realize that we and ours can be a part of that or not. When this was all over, Abraham understood how important his life was to the generations following. It's vital for us to understand how important our lives are to those that follow us.

Abraham- A Servant's Heart!

Scriptures references:
Genesis 18:2,6 And he lifts up his eyes and looked and lo, three men stood by him: and when he saw them, he ran to meet them from the tent door, and bowed himself toward the ground. Abraham hastened into the tent unto Sarah and said Make ready quickly three measures of fine meal, knead it and make cakes upon the hearth.

Genesis 17:21 18:1, 3-8	1 Corinthians 2:14
Genesis 18:9-15 19:1	Hebrews 13:2
Romans 11:29	Revelations 2:1

    Genesis 18 contains such powerful things. I pray God will give us a complete revelation of it in its entirety. If we should by any means lose or leave anything out, we will be grieved. There are revelations that will come to us as we continue down this pilgrimage. God has called us a special generation to serve out this dispensation of grace and mercy. We are enriched and thank God for that.

    The sovereignty of man is such a vast subject that I desire to know more about it. There are some great prophetic overtones as we walk out a preview of an hour to come. Now we are living in that hour. It is wonderful that God has given us this time to live, but we must take advantage of it. To do that we must have an understanding of what God is saying and what He is doing here in Genesis 18.

Genesis 18:1-3 And the Lord speared unto him in the plains of Mamre: and he sat in the tent door in the heat of the day; And he lifts up his eyes and looked and lo, three men stood by him: and when he saw them, he ran to meet them from the tent door and bowed himself toward the ground, And said, My Lord, if now I have found favor in thy sight, pass not away, I pray thee, from thy servant:

Abraham is sitting in the tent door that day and sees three angels coming. The Bible does not tell us how he knows they are Angels. In Genesis 19, two of these angels go on to Sodom and Gomorrah. When the two get to Sodom and Gomorrah, we learn that Lot, who is one of the rulers or judges that sits at the gate, recognizes the two that were coming even as did Abraham. He knew they were angelical beings. However, everyone else in Sodom and Gomorrah and the other three sister cities could not recognize them as angelical beings. Therefore, this is a mystery. I believe there was a spirit of discernment.

Why is it that Abraham and Lot could discern that these men were of God, angelical beings, yet they did eat and drink, as Jesus did after His resurrection? But the world could not see them as Angels.

Isn't it amazing that Abraham could see they were angels from afar? The spirit of discernment was operating in these men's lives. The Bible says in Hebrews that some entertain angels unaware, but these men were aware these men were angelical beings.

Hebrews 13:2 Be not forgetful to entertain strangers: for thereby some have entertained angels unawares.

I wonder what gifts God gives us that we are not aware of that we need to utilize spiritually. Down through the years when pastors would come, and my father-in-law would shake their hand, he would say, "That old boy is all right," or "That fellow is not!" I never saw him miss it. My mother also had discernment about her and I never knew her to miss it either. There is something about the spiritual entity about an individual, but we know the Bible says that the natural mind cannot conceive spiritual things.

Who Are the Sons of the Promise?

1 Corinthians 2:14 But the natural man receiveth not the things of the Spirit of God: for they are foolishness unto him: neither can he know them, because they are spiritually discerned.

So, no one can teach us about discernment, only the Lord can give us this gift... it is not something learned.

Every one of us is born with a purpose and a calling. There are gifts and there are spiritual callings. A gift is something that you can do better than the other person; it is a gifting to do a particular thing. Most country singers started out in the house of God. God gifted them to sing. Someday they will have to answer for that gift and how they used it.

Spiritual callings are the apostles, pastors, teachers, evangelists, etc. In other words, God has called me to preach the Gospel, and I will be held accountable for how I used it. God will not take back His gifts or callings, and He will not change his mind. You can use them or not; it is up to you.

Romans 11:29 For the gifts and calling of God are without repentance.

I will be judged for how I used this gift. If I backslide, I would go to a devil's hell. I am a free agent. I would not go there just as a sinner, I would go there as a back sliding Pentecostal Preacher.

Some people use their gifts for God, and others do not. There is a difference in gifts and callings. Some people just have them and I do not understand it. It is beautiful to see someone do something for God whether they are called or not.

Nevertheless, I do know that Abraham and Lot did

recognize these men as Angels. We are learning about the dividing line of Abraham and Lot! Between apostasy and the father of the sons of promise! Like David and Rebekah, Abraham had a servant's heart.

Did God ask David to fight Goliath?

No, because he was a man ready to do what God needed him to do.

Did Eliezer ask Rebekah to give water to him and the camels?

No, because she had a servant's heart and was ready to do what she needed to do. Abraham had a servant's heart that showed up in spiritual things and material things. Sometimes we as Christians will pinch every penny that we give to God and blow it in other areas.

When Abraham and Lot separated, there was confusion and the herdsmen were arguing among themselves. Abraham showed us a servant's heart. Abraham told Lot to choose which way he wanted to go and he would go the other. If any one had the right to pick which way he wanted to go, it was Abraham. He could have said, "Brother-in-law, you go that way and we will go this way," but he did not because he had a servant's heart.

We should say, "Lord let me do it." Whatever our hands find to do, we should do it. We will be rewarded in the world to come. The response in our hearts to God's call will enlarge our kingdom. What we are prior to the Holy Ghost, and what we are after the Holy Ghost is a noticeable difference!

This is an interesting observation:

You will notice that when Christ came, in His hour, He washed the disciple's feet. Now in this setting when these three Angels came to Abraham, he made provisions for them and brought them water for them

Who Are the Sons of the Promise?

to wash their own feet.

There is an order of servants that goes beyond Abraham; he will not be the Bride Hood order.

John the Baptist is not the Bride Hood order; they are friends to the Bride Groom. We can be the Bride Hood order if we take the servants position to its fullest and most complete order.

As humble servants of Christ, we deny ourselves.

Therefore, Abraham did have a servant's heart for his hour. When he saw these angels coming, he asked Sarah to make three fine meals for them.

Genesis 18:6 And Abraham hastened into the tent unto Sarah, and said Make ready quickly three measures of fine meal, knead it, and make cakes upon the hearth.

Abraham did not ask the angels if it would be alright, nor did he ask them if they wanted him to fix them something to eat. I was surprised they ate it!

This is one time Abraham took the rulership of the home. Abraham went into the tent and instructed Sarah to prepare three measures of fine flour.

Now here is salvation, sanctification, and the Holy Ghost.

Genesis 18:7 And Abraham ran unto the herd and fetched a calf tender and good, and gave it unto a young man; and he hasted to dress it.

Abraham commanded his servants to kill the best calf and dress it. He wanted God to have the best. We also want God to have the best that we have. Whenever I'm too old to give Him anything, then I can retire. As long as I can give God something, I want God to have the best.

Genesis 18:8 And he took butter, and milk, and the calf which he had dressed, and set it before them; and he stood by them under the tree, and they did eat.

Abraham brought in his best and presented it before the angels, and they did eat.

The heavenly visitation that came to Abraham under the law was three angelical beings. Abraham submitted, bowed to the earth, and they came and ate with him.

The heavenly visitation that comes to us is of the Holy Ghost. When you and I are submissive to the Holy Ghost, He takes His abode in us. We must have the reverence of God and we must respect God. We can grieve the Holy Ghost. He will not be led to us and He will not come upon us unless we must make Him the honored guest in our lives. We can come face to face with angelical beings prior to the rapture or prior to our ascending and facing the Judgment Seat of Christ. The Judgment Seat of Christ will be the first thing that happens after we leave this order, after the sun has sat on our human pilgrimage, when we have completed our journey here, not the Marriage Supper of the Lamb. The Judgment Seat of Christ is the position that Christ takes so we can be rewarded for the work we did for Him on earth, while we were flesh and blood. Right then and there, Christ will determine on what level we will serve throughout eternity – 10 fold, 20 fold, 30 fold, 60 fold, 90 fold, or 100 fold.

Now as soon as the angels had eaten, they said let us talk about the church.

The first thing they said after they ate is, "Where is Sarah?" Sarah represents the Church.

In other words, let us talk about you and the Church! The first thing that you and I will face when we come to the Judgment Seat of Christ is what happened in our

Who Are the Sons of the Promise?

relationship to His Church.

- How did the Church conceive from you? Did it or did it not?

- Did you make a difference in the Church?

- Were you in an imitate Relationship and did you enlarge the Church? Why not?

This will determine our judgment place for eternity. When we face God, our pastor will be by our side to give an account for what they taught us and we will give an account on what we did with that teaching. How are you and the Church doing? Are you faithful? Has your commitment to the Church caused sons and daughters to be born? The angel said, "Abraham, sit down and let's talk about the Church." This act represents our responsibility and commitment to the Church, supporting her financially and physically and being involved. There are many preachers and many people in the Church world today, but the Church is not conceiving from them, because they are still in the flesh. His Church cannot conceive from the flesh, only from the spirit. The Spirit of God working in us will bring conception in the Church, and the Church will be enlarged or grow and have a man-child. The principles will be reinstated in the Church and the Church will give birth to a son.

These angels came for two reasons:

- They came to talk about a man-child.

- They came to destroy Sodom and Gomorrah.

Genesis 17:21 But my covenant will I establish with Isaac, which Sarah shall bear unto thee at this set time in the next year.

God told Abraham that Sarah will have a son and it will

be by this time next year. The angel relayed the very same message. These messages needed to be close together. When Abraham lifted up his eyes, how many men did he see coming? There were three men coming….

Genesis 19:1 And there came two angels to Sodom at even; Three angels came to Abraham's tent, and only two Angels went to Sodom; we have lost an Angel.

What happened to the other angel?

Where did he go and what is he doing?

Genesis 18:9-12 And they said unto him, where is Sarah thy wife? And he said behold in the tent. And he said, I will certainly return unto thee according to the time of life and lo, Sarah thy wife shall have a son. And Sarah heard it in the tent door, which was behind him. Now Abraham and Sarah were old and well stricken in age; and it ceased to be with Sarah after the manner of women. Therefore Sarah laughed within herself saying, after I am waxed old shall I have pleasure, my Lord being old also?

Did the angel need Abraham to tell him where Sarah was?

No, he did not!

Sometimes Sarah is submissive, and other times she was not. However, Sarah called Abraham "Lord" as an act of submission. Later Abraham takes Isaac to Mount Mariah to offer him as a sacrifice. If Sarah had not been submissive, she could have caused some problems. We visualize Sarah when she offered Hagar to Abram, as being a woman in charge of her home, as most women are in charge of the home. However, as we look further, we realize this is divine providence.

The angel asked, "Where is Sarah thy wife?" Abraham replied, "She is in the tent."

The scriptures teach us that she was not only in the tent, but she was also listening to the conversation when the Angel said, "According to the time of life Sarah is unable to conceive. Nevertheless, she will have a son by this time next year." When Sarah heard this she laughed! She laughed within herself; she did not break out in laughter.

She was not lying later when the angel said you laughed. She laughed within herself! The response from the angel was, "Is anything too hard for God?" This also lets us know that God is concerned about our thought life.

Genesis 18:13 And the Lord said unto Abraham, Wherefore did Sarah laugh, saying, Shall I of a surety bear a child, which am old?

Scripture teaches us that Sarah was laughing because she could not possibly understand how she could bear a child at 90 years of age.

Is providence in this?

I believe that providence is here and will show us something that is yet to happen in the man-child and the judgments of God. There is the written Word and then there is the written Word that takes on a deeper level. The Word has more than one level and one definition in completion.

Sodom and Gomorrah were destroyed before Sarah gives birth to Isaac, the man-child.

The flesh is the reason that the man-child was born on the wrong side of Sodom's tribulation.

**Why did the angels tell Sarah she was going to have

a son and not a daughter?

The covenant needs to be in the man, in his name, and in his blood.

What does the man always symbolize?

He symbolizes the principles. Now today the Church has fewer principles, and anything goes. We have lost our principles. The Church has embraced it all – some are sipping, dipping, and some are gambling. However, the true Church of our Lord Jesus Christ will not be compromised.

In the seven letters to the seven churches of Asia, theologians cannot decide whether they were angelical beings or they were pastors to the church.

"And unto the Angel of the Church of Ephesus write these things"... Revelations 2:1

The Greek word means the same, whether referring to an angelic being or someone in the natural flesh. The subject is a message from God.

In the scriptures that refer to the angel at Sardis or to the angel at the Church of Philadelphia, or to the angel at the Church of Laodicea, it is simply referring to the individual that is going to give the message; it does not matter whether it is an Angel or a pastor. The person does not matter; it is the message that counts and the message is from God. The men that visited Abraham were angels and these angels had a message from God.

Abraham with Justice & Judgment

Scripture references:
Genesis 18:20,21 And the Lord said, Because the cry of Sodom and Gomorrah is great, and because their sin is very grievous; I will go down now and see whether they have done altogether according to the cry of it, which is come unto me; and if not I will know.
Genesis 4:10   1 Corinthians 3:13,14,15
Acts 2:16,39   1 Peter 1:17

    Sometimes we are so caught up in things of life that we have a tendency to forget that the only thing on the face of this earth that God is going to save is His people, and the rest of the world is going to burn. That tells us that every individual is very important, and we thank God for the fact that He loves us that much. We have seen a providential act of God, and there are some things in this event that I am still waiting for Him to reveal.

    There is a parallel between the three angels that came to Abraham's tent and the things that transpired around this event. This story has a great deal of prophetic overtones. In fact, everything we have studied about Abraham has prophetic overtones. One thing I am not clear on is the sequence of events.

    Having studied the Book of Revelation, I often wonder in what order these events occur. In the event with the three angels is the first mention of his name. Isaac and Abraham portray a certain order of people.

Genesis 18:17,18,19 And the Lord said, Shall I Hide from Abraham that thing which I do; Seeing that Abraham shall surely become a great and mighty nation, and all the nations of the earth shall be blessed in him? For I know him, that he will command his children and his household after him, and they shall keep the way of the Lord, to do justice and judgment; that the Lord may bring upon Abraham that which he hath spoken of him

God says, "I know him!"

We have just learned that Sarah had laughed within herself. That was an inside chuckle and God knew it. He knows the intent of the heart does He not? Now He is saying that He knows Abraham. He knows that he is going to become great and he will bless all the nations of the world. Nevertheless, He also says something here that really caught my attention. He is going to do justice and judgment, and in doing justice and judgment, he is going to be teaching My commandments unto the children and to his household after him. When Abraham does these three things, God will be able to fulfill His promises to Him.

Now, if Abraham's heart was not fixed on doing these three things and God knowing his heart, then the promises of God would be nullified to a great degree. However, because God knew that he was going to teach his children and his household, justice and judgments, God could then complete what He wanted to do in his life and in the life of his children.

This is saying many things. One thing that God is saying here is if we do not bring our children up in the ways of the Lord, then that stops God's blessings that flows to that child.

Acts 2:16,39 But this is that which was spoken by the prophet Joel; For the promise is unto you and to your children and to all that is afar off, even as many as the Lord our God shall call.

God's promise is not just an individual promise to

you or me. This is the reason the Bible says there is a way that a man can be sanctified and a way that a wife can be sanctified, and God's promise is not just to that one Christian that is in that home. He said the husband can be sanctified through the wife and the wife can be sanctified through the husband, and the children can be sanctified through the parents. Therefore we have to open our lives up for God's blessings to be upon our family, our children and our children's children. God is saying here as the angels are talking together, that Abraham will do it, so now He can fulfill everything He has promised him. Abraham's obedience opened the door for the blessings to flow.

Is it not wonderful that God gives us that opportunity to open that door?

We can open that door to our children and grandchildren unto the third and fourth generation away.

That will happen by us not showing partiality and teaching the commandments of God and not just justice, but judgment also. This is a wonderful promise to our children, our family and us.

Genesis 18:20,21 And the Lord said, because the cry of Sodom and Gomorrah is great and because their sin is very grievous; I will go down now and see whether they have done altogether according to the cry of it, which is come unto me; and if not, I will know.

Many times the world thinks that sin does not have a voice, but sin has a voice. God said "the cry of Sodom and Gomorrah has come to me." It was not a cry of deliverance or forgiveness, it was not a cry for more Churches; it was a cry of sin.

Do you remember what God said to Cain when he slew Abel?

Genesis 4:10 And he said, What hast thou done? the voice of thy brother's blood crieth unto me from the ground.

Here the angel is saying that the cry of sin of Sodom and Gomorrah has been heard, and he has come down to see. I appreciate God's approach to things. He did not have to come and see. He knew. Just like so many things, He knows and He is all knowledge and omnipresence. Man is a part of this thing and God came down for man's sake. The cry of sin has been heard, and He sent these angels down. He knew that Israel was going to reject his Son; he knew that they were going to crucify Him.

So why did God send Jesus down to be rejected by Israel?

Why did God send Jesus down knowing that they were going to crucify Him?

He knew that they were going to beat His back and pluck His beard, spit in His face. He knew all those things, did He not?

In fact, it was prophesied that they would do that, but you see, we all have to have that tree to be judged and develop moral character. Therefore, these men in Sodom and Gomorrah were going to have to give voice to these angels and then they would not be guiltless before God. They would know that they were guilty of what they had done. We cannot be judged unless we have the opportunity to choose.

If God knows the end from the beginning, then what order of predestination is that?

It is not God's fault this world has come to the state of affairs that it is in. The Bible has promised us that if we would each one take our position as parents that this world would be saved. But because we flake off and take a course of lesser resistance and the luring lights pull us away from commitment, then our children are not under that umbrella of coming back to God because they were raised right. Dads are off doing their thing, Mothers are off doing their thing, and the children are doing their thing and that is anything they want. Then these children are not under an umbrella, so they have children and all of this is outside of God's umbrella. If my wife and I follow the way of grace and mercy and the way God has intended for us to, then there will be no room out there, the latitude and longitude for the devil.

There are children in this world that do not even know the name of Jesus.

So, whose fault is it? God's fault?

No, it is our fault and God knew that we would take the course of lesser resistance if we could. We took it and our children are lost. Understand that everything brings forth after its own kind.

• If I am a disobedient churchgoer, guess what I am going to raise?
• If I am a Christian that only comes one hour a week, guess what my Children are going to do?

This is cause and effect, sowing and reaping. We do not need to expect anybody that we are raising to be any more holy or righteous than we are. This world has gotten out of control because we quit doing God's will, and anyone that goes this route will end up down in that pit.

We hear people today saying that if God loves people so much, where is He?

In addition, God is saying, "Where is My Church? I gave them authority to do that." Just because God knows the beginning and the end, do not let that bother you. What needs to bother you is your work for God!

1 Corinthians 3:13,14,15 Every man's work shall be made manifest: for the day shall declare it, because it shall be revealed by fire; and the fire shall try every man's work of what sort it is. If any man's work abide which he hath built thereupon, he shall receive a reward. If any man's work shall be burned, he shall suffer loss: but he himself shall be saved; yet so as by fire.

What Paul is simply saying is that we choose what work we do. We choose whether we work for God or we go out here and play around doing whatever the flesh wants to do. We decide that.

Whatever we did today, that is our works. We are what we do, so when life is over, all that I have done, day after day, will be tried by the fires of eternity.

And if it burns then I have suffered loss, because time is a precious commodity that God has given us to lay up treasures in heaven, to be rulers over cities and nations. If everything burns, then I have suffered loss, though I myself might be saved, as the thief on the cross, the last hour of repentance. Therefore, predestination and why we have to go through it, is because we have an eternity and it will be forever and ever. As a whole, I can say it this way, but there are exceptions to the rule. God promises that your family will be saved, if we are obedient and faithful, but He does not promise your family a reward. He will save your family and it may be on their deathbed, because they have a free will and it may be in the last hour. He does not promise them a great reward, that is up to them. However, He can promise you that they will be saved.

Acts 16:31 And they said, Believe on the Lord Jesus Christ, and thou shalt be saved and thy house.
Our rewards are going to be individually and our eternities will be individual. God has promised me that He would save my household, but He did not promise me that they would get a great reward in heaven. Rewards are

giving for what we do on this earth for God. In addition, I reiterate here, that is why time is a great precious commodity for us, so we can lay up treasures in Heaven. I leave you with this scripture:

1 Peter 1:17 And if ye call on the Father, who without respect of persons judgeth according to every man's work, pass the time of your sojourning here in fear.

The Sodomy of Sodom!

Scripture references:
Genesis 19:1,17 And there came two angels to Sodom at even; and Lot sat in the gate of Sodom: and Lot seeing them rose up to meet them; and he bowed himself with his face toward the ground.
Escape for thy life; look not behind thee, neither stay thou in all the plain; escape to the mountains lest thou be consumed.

Genesis 19:2,3,4,18	Romans 1:18-32
Genesis 19:19,20,22,23	1 Corinthians 6: 9-10
Psalms 66:18	Hebrews 11:5
John 9:31	James 4:17

We have a very interesting lesson today.

This is a very vital time of understanding. It seems like if there were a lesson that I would not want to miss, it would be this one. These are very enlightening moments that God established in His Word so that you and I living in this hour would not be ignorant. But that we would be knowledgeable about the vices of the adversary and the consequences of sin and the hope of redemption.

There are many people that are living on grace, their works are not pleasing God. Many of us Christians are living totally on grace. We have not purposed in our heart to go on to perfection, laying not again the foundation of dead works in repentance. Therefore, we are looking in the 19th chapter of Genesis. At this time, we have learned that the three angels have come to Abraham's tent and he has made intercession for the people who lived in Sodom and Gomorrah.

Two angels have gone on to Sodom, and Lot saw them coming. Lot's position here most feel like he was an official; a judge and he sat the gate of the city. Much is symbolized about the gate of a city...

Genesis 19:1 And there came two angels to Sodom at even; and Lot sat in the gate of Sodom: and Lot seeing them rose up to meet them; and he bowed himself with his face toward the ground;

Why did he say evening?

We are in the evening of grace and mercy in this hour. Did you notice that Gomorrah was not mentioned here? Now, here He is just talking about Sodom. Let us start with sodomy and it will destroy the whole city.

Lot sat at the gate of the city, and he recognized them as angels as they came toward him. About the gatekeeper, much is said and symbolized about the gate of a city.

When Jacob and others prayed for their descendants, they would say, "May they occupy the gate of the city," and when they got into warfare they would say, "Might you occupy the gate of your enemy's city."

So occupying the gate meant that you were in control of the city. Whoever controlled the city sat at the gate, the city's fathers would meet at the gate and judge many of the domestic problems and so forth and so on...

Therefore, Lot was a judge or one that was a part of the judicial order in the city of Sodom.

Genesis 19:22,23 Haste thee; escape thither; for I cannot do anything till thou be come hither. Therefore, the name of the city was called Zoar. The sun risen upon the earth when Lot entered into Zoar.

The angel says to Lot, "I have to get you out of the city, because I cannot bring judgment upon this city until you get out." So here is a picture of an order of people who qualify to come out before the judgment. Moreover, that angel rehearsed that in Lot's hearing, "I cannot bring judgment on this city unto you get out." Nowhere has God ever poured out his wrath on His people!

So those that miss the rapture and are not accounted worthy to leave here, I am not saying that there is not going to be Christians left here; there will not be any obedient Christian here. The disobedient has to learn the wisdom of the just.

The city of Sodom has been visited by these two angels and now they are at Lot's home and the men of the city have learned that there are two strangers in town and because they are people of sodomy…(think about this)… they have come for these two men!

Genesis 19:2,3,4 And he said," Behold now, my lords, turn in, I pray you, into your servant's house, and tarry all night and wash your feet and ye shall rise up early and go on your ways. And they said, Nay; but we will abide in the street all night.

And he pressed upon them greatly; and they turned in unto him and entered into his house; and he made them a feast and did bake unleavened bread, and they did eat.

But before they lay down, the men of the city even the men of Sodom, compassed the house round, both old and young, all the people from every quarter:

Lot says that he does not want to turn these men over to them. He pleaded with them. This city had come to the place where they were more interested in perversion than they were even as men interested in virgins. Lot offers his two daughters who are at home and who are virgins to these men outside, and those men were not interested in those two virgins. They were only interested in men. Therefore, sodomy had taken this kind of a hold on this town of Sodom. While Lot was pleading with these men, one of the angels reached out and pulled Lot back inside, and the angel smote the balance with blindness so they could not find the door and they left off what they were doing. We are now talking about the sin count of Sodom.

1 Corinthians 6:9-10 Know ye not that the unrighteous shall not inherit the kingdom of God? Be not deceiver: neither fornicators, nor idolaters, nor adulterers, nor effeminate, nor abusers of themselves with mankind. Nor thieves, nor covetous, nor drunkards, nor revilers, nor extortioners, shall inherit the kingdom of God.

We are living in an hour where women are rejecting womanhood and men are rejecting their manhood. Our women want to look like men and our men want to look like women. Many are doing this in ignorance and some are doing this in rebellion. They do not want to project the image that God has created them in. Women were given to us veiled, they do not like to be veiled, and so they want to act like the men. Men do not want the responsibility of the principles of life, the home; they want to cast off to the women to raise the children They will just leave the mothers to raise them. They are rejecting manhood, and so they begin to look like women. They begin to hang ornaments on them and they look like they have fallen into someone's tackle box. All of this is because of the day and the hour that we are living in and that is a sad commentary. There are many questions about the homosexuals. In addition, there are many questions about lesbians.

We want to touch lightly on this, because our study, this lesson, is on the sodomy of Sodom. Why God despises it and why God brought judgment prematurely. He did not destroy the whole world like He did with the flood, but he is telling us of God's thoughts concerning this type of sin.

Paul tells us in Corinthians that we will not enter into the kingdom.

This is the sin the Bible speaks about that will go to the third and fourth generation, no one is born a homosexual or lesbian. I want to show you where homosexual and lesbians comes from. This brought the judgment of God once and it will bring it again.

Romans 1:18 For the wrath of God is revealed from heaven against all ungodliness and unrighteousness of men, who hold the truth in unrighteousness;

They know the truth, but they live unrighteous. They think that have found hope but they are holding the truth in an unrighteous life and there is no hope there. To the sinner all things are sin. God hears and regardeth not the prayers of the sinner, unless it is a repentive prayer.

John 9:31 Now we know that God heareth not sinners: but if any man be a worshiper of God and doeth his will, him he heareth.

We hear often people who will say, "I'll be praying for you," but they are living an unrighteous life. This person in particular I heard, was living with a man that she is not married to, therefore God will not hear her prayers. She saw the need for prayer, but she was holding it in unrighteousness. The scriptures further say:

Psalms 66:18 If I regard inequity in my heart, the Lord will not hear me:

What is the reason or how do people become

perverted?

They know who God is and they know what the truth is. They know sin and righteousness. They know that others doing what I am doing is in rebellion. When we know the truth and continue to do that, it becomes rebellion to us.

James 4:17 Therefore, to Him that knoweth to do good and doeth it not, to him it is sin.

If I know to do good and do not, then I am holding the truth in unrighteousness.

Do you think that these young people today really know the truth, has it been handed down?

This sin will go to the third and fourth generation, everything brings forth after its kind. God put this law in motion in the Garden of Eden. So, my children may commit the same sin I am committing, and they may be ignorant of it to a degree, but the consequences are still there.

So to sum this up...
• I know the will of God.
• I know what is right.
• I know what is glamorizing the flesh; I know what is crucifying the flesh.

I know what is right and I do not want to do that, and the Church has embraced that!

John the Revelator was pastoring the Church at Ephesus and God told the Church after John had pastured there an undisclosed number of years, you need to repent and do your first works over again. You see it is never your or my sin until we approve it. If I know what living a holy life is and I will not do it, my sons will be worse than I am. However, if I do exactly what God has called me to do, and they will follow me willfully, then they will reach more people than I will. So you see it goes both directions here. God has established the order that we will live and we will either follow God's laws or we will break them. The choice is ours and there are consequences for each decision we make.

Romans 1:28,29,30,32 And even as they did not like to retain God in their knowledge, God gave them over to a reprobate mind, to do those things, which are not convenient; Being filled with all unrighteousness, fornication, wickedness, covetousness, maliciousness; full of envy, murder, debate, deceit, malignity; whisperers, backbiters, haters of God, despiteful, proud, boasters, inventors of evil things, disobedient to parents. Who knowing the judgment of God, that they which commit such things are worthy of death, not only do the same, but have pleasure in them that do them.

Now do you notice in that list God does not mention adultery?

Nevertheless, He does mention fornication. Fornication is any sexual perversion, adultery is man and woman, but fornication is any sexual sin contrary and outside the boundaries that God has set forth. That is another reason that I think when we come together, we need to recognize the importance and give God the glory and praise for everything in our lives.

Praising God is an antidote against this sin. We know who God is. We know what He has done for us, and I am not ashamed to give God the glory in everything. Do not confuse our position on this matter. God receives praise, thanks, and glory for all He has done.

Myths concerning homosexuality taken by a national

survey:

- It is a natural thing!

It is not a natural thing by God's standard.

(Read Romans 1:18-32.)

Only 2% of homosexuals and lesbians that we have a record of reach the age of 65. Today life expectancy is around 73-74.

Therefore, this is not a healthy, natural, or normal lifestyle.

The average male, who is a homosexual lives to 38 years.

The average female that is a lesbian lives to be 45 years old.

- There are 10% to 12% of our nation are homosexuals and lesbians.

According to this same survey, there are only 5% to 6% of our nation that is of the gay lifestyle. There are more homosexual male, 2.8 %.... than female, 1.4%.... So that is 4 to 5 % of America's population at this time.

- The homosexual lifestyle is irreversible.

This is not true; there are thousands of people who Jesus Christ has saved.

He has washed them in His blood, and cleansed them, has put them out here in a normal life, and has set them free.

People who are taken up in this sin feel that there is no hope, but there is.

First they have to recognize that they have this sin, and want to be delivered. God will not invade their privacy or my privacy and over ride our free will in this. This is why we must teach people that this is a spiritual sin It is the effect of someone who has let down on their commitment to God and   drifted down into this area of sin.

We need to look at God's program and see what we are doing here, and why this is a spiritual sin. Because not only do we know who God is and do not give Him the glory, but it is more than that. God set the standard up for husband and wife and spoke to them to replenish the earth. Once to Adam and then again told Noah after the flood to replenish the earth. God has set forth this means on how the earth is to be replenished and how to have continual bloodline and birth. When we break that order and when the Church, who is a type of the woman, refuses to take the seed, which is the Word of God, and nurture it within us and hand back to him one of his kind, we no longer have a reason to exist.

This is why it is a spiritual sin...

God ordained that the woman would receive the seed from the man, nurture that, and hand back one of his kind to him. The only woman in the world that had the right to reproduce my kind was the woman who I was joined together in holy matrimony and holy wedlock. She then had the right to reproduce my kind and hand them back to me.

The Church is God's woman and the Word of God is His seed and the Holy Ghost is the administrator. We must receive this in our hearts, we must nurture this, and hand Him back one like Himself. Unless we produce Christians, unless they are Christ like, then what purpose does the Church have? God ordained purpose of our living, purpose of our being. I have often said one of the saddest things in the world is for a person to live a lifetime and never know why they were living. We have been placed here to reproduce His kind and that is what we must do. When the woman loses her desire to reproduce his kind, it is the Church that has lost their desire to reach the lost, and that is a sad commentary. When the men are no longer interested in living the principles of God's word, so that the women can pattern their lives after the leader of the home, then to us that is a sad commentary. Therefore, that is why this is a spiritual sin, we take the natural and do that is not natural and God has sent judgment to Sodom, because of that.

Genesis 19:17,18,19 And it came to pass, when they had brought them forth abroad, that he said, Escape for thy life; look not behind thee, neither stay thou in all the plain; escape to the mountain, lest thou be consumed. And Lot said unto them, Oh, not so, my Lord: Behold now, thy servant hath found grace in thy sight, and thou hast magnified thy mercy, which thou hast showed unto me in saving thy life; and I cannot escape to the mountain, lest some evil take me, and I die:

We are seeing the setting of Noah verses Enoch and Lot verses Abraham. Enoch was translated and Noah went through the flood.

Why was Noah not translated?

Why was he not raptured?

The Bible tells us that Enoch has this testimony that he pleased God. He had this testimony before he was taken away, that he pleased God.

Hebrews 11:5 By faith, Enoch was translated that he should not see death; and was not found, because God had translated him: for before his translation he had this testimony, that he pleased God.

That is a picture of the bride wanting to please the husband. The Bible tells us that Noah found grace in the eyes of the Lord. Now compare the difference in pleasing God verses grace…

• Noah found grace and he went through the flood.
• Enoch pleased God and taken out before the Flood.

So, the Angels said "Lot flee for you lives, Lot go to the mountains" and Lot said, "I do not want to go to the mountains, I want to go to Zoar!"

Genesis 19:20 Behold now, this city near to flee unto, and it is a little one: Oh, let me escape thither, (is it not a little one) and my soul shall live.

You can measure a person by their desires and if Lot had desired to leave as the angels had instructed him, he would not have lost all he had. First of all, he was in the wrong place at the wrong time and he chose to go that direction. Now God said, "Come and go to the mountains." Lot said, "No, I do not want to do that!" Therefore, it cost him everything that he had.

He became the father of incest, which is the sin just prior to homosexuality.

In addition, lunar and lunatic is the sin that follows homosexuality. Lot is going where he wants to go. This scares me when I see my people telling me what they want to do and I see them doing exactly what they want, rather than what God wants them to do.

Therefore I leave you with this…

Notice that there were five cities that were called the plain cities and God did spare the one that Lot was in, but that was the only one that was spared…

Lot Lingered & Lot's Salvation

Scripture references:
Genesis 19:27,28 And Abraham gat up early in the morning to the place where he stood before the Lord: And he looked toward Sodom and Gomorrah, and toward all the land of the plain, and beheld and lo, the smoke of the country went up as the smoke of a furnace.

Genesis 19:15,18
Genesis 19:20-38
Matthew 1:5,6
Luke 9:62

Hebrews 5:8,9,12
Revelation 12:1,2,5,6
Revelation 1:9

We are all humanized, and the world that we live in has an affect on us. Insomuch that we have spent a measure of ourselves to buy, build, and to have. All this affects us. This all started by talking about the sons of promise. Nevertheless, I want to show you that Lot can thank Abraham for his salvation and he can blame himself for the fact that he lost everything he had. The very fact that he was tied into stuff cost him everything he had. Now he was a believer and we will learn more about that, why Lot was even spared. However, no thanks to Lot, he and his family got out of there.

Ponder these questions in your heart:

In the world we live in, how attached are we to things? How much emphasis and value are we placing on these things?

Also, I contend that we need to look at this lesson and if the things that we have accumulated keep us from being obedient to God today, they will keep us from making the rapture this evening.

Genesis 19:15,16 And when the morning arose, then the angels hastened Lot saying, Arise, take thy wife, and thy two daughters, which are here; lest thou be consumed in the iniquity of the city.

And while he lingered, the men laid hold upon his hand, and upon the hand of his wife, and upon the hand of his two daughters; the Lord being merciful unto him: and they brought him forth, and set him without the city.

The angel of the Lord told Lot to get his wife and two daughters out, but they did not go. Finally, the Angels reached out, took each of them by the hand, and brought them out. They did not come on their own. While Lot was lingering, the angel said, "Go," but he still lingered. The reason Lot was living in Sodom in the first place was he never found a servant's heart. The word "angel" means "messenger from God." In this particular setting, it was an angelical being. The Word of God comes to us by the providential act of God and by the printed Word of God. This is the will of God. How much value do we place on that? I think it necessary to evaluate our lives and ask, "How do I choose obedience to God?" It is not about what the pastor, superintendent, or anyone else thinks, but a personal knowledge of God's requirements of me. This has a much deeper meaning than what I am able to explain to you today. Lot lingered, and the Angel grabbed Lot, wife, and two daughters by the hand and drug him out of Sodom. Perhaps he would have been better off to have them left there. The world would have been better off. Nothing good comes out of Lot. This is a sad commentary, and all this because he had not found a servant's heart. Most adversaries that Israel confronted when they were coming out of Egypt were Lot's descendents. They had to go many miles out of their way on their journey because of Lot's descents and they went without water and food because of Lot's descendants.

Therefore, if our lives here are not going to make it better for those that follow, what good am I being here?

When our life is over, hopefully our efforts will make this place a better place to live. When the children of Israel were crossing the wilderness, they ran into Lot's descendents, and they said, "Let us buy some water, let us buy some bread." They said, "Not only, can you not buy water and bread of us, you cannot even cross the land." You have Lot to thank for that because he made that decision on the mountain. His attitude of "I want what I want" caused everyone to pay the price. It was because of Abraham that God saved Lot!

Genesis 19:17 And it came to pass, when they had brought them forth abroad, that he said, escape for thy life; look not behind thee, neither stay thou in all the plain; escape to the mountain, lest thou be consumed.

Why did God instruct Lot, Lot's wife, and Lot's two daughters to not look back, but it was alright for Abraham to stand there and watch it?

Abraham stood there, looked on while the cities burned, and shook his head. He probably was thinking, "I prayed for those people, I counseled with God for those people, I did my best for those people, but I refuse to be a part of them." Abraham could stand and watch it. There are many things we will see from a lofty summit that many people will see first hand, and we will look at it very differently than they looked at it.

Genesis 19:18 And Lot said unto them, Oh, not so, my Lord:

People who do not have a servant's heart are confused. The angel brought Lot and his people out and said, "Now, flee to the mountain." Then Lot turns and says, "Wait a minute. I do not want to go to the mountain." That sounds like people today who say, "I do not want to go to Sunday school class; there is nothing that they can teach me because I am smarter than everyone there. There is nothing that I can learn, so I do not need to go." These who say this are blind.

Lot says, "No, no, I will not go there." He is debating the matter with the angel that dragged him out of the fire. You would think that anyone would have enough sense to not debate the matter with this man. Lot said, "Wait a minute. I want to go over to this little city." He was confused on the mountain, he was confused in Sodom, he was confused about getting out of there. He had not made the commitment.

The confusion began when he insisted to this angel that he go to Zoar. When he arrived he was baffled, confused, and bewildered. Finally he called the family together and said, "Hey, let's get out of here and go to the mountain." That is exactly where the angel told him to go in the first place. Lot went to the mountain but was confused. Selfish people will never put a lasting smile on their face. They will never be happy, and no one can ever make them happy. It is one of those unfortunate things that the devil has blinded us with, as he deceived mother Eve.

When Eve saw that the fruit was pleasant to her eye and it was good to her taste, she took it and became the most miserable person in the world until the day of her death. This is what happened to brother Lot. He was not happy in Zoar, and so he goes to the mountain.

Genesis 19:20,23,26 Behold now this city is near to flee unto, and it is a little one: Oh, let me escape thither, (is it not a little one?) and my soul shall live. The sun was risen upon the earth when Lot entered into Zoar. (Zoar means

Who Are the Sons of the Promise?

little one) But his wife looked back from behind him, and she became a pillar of salt.

Therefore, it seems they have now entered the city of Zoar. I always had in my minds eye, that as Lot and Lot's wife and the two daughters were leaving Sodom, they traveled just a little ways out of town when Lot's wife looked back.

However, here it says that they were in the city of Zoar and then Lot's wife looked back. I had not noticed that before. Only when he arrived in Zoar did God rain down fire on Sodom, so Lot has to be in Zoar to see this happen.

No matter where we are, there is no need to be looking back.

Luke 9:62 And Jesus said unto him, No man, having put his hands to the plough and looking back, is fit for the kingdom of God.

When I hear people testifying and telling what they did while they were in sin, it seems they wish they were still there. What happened to me while I was in sin just showed my ignorance and how foolish I was. I do not want to advertise it, because that just looks bad on me. We do not want to look back, not ever! If we are not careful, we will be lured back into things of sin. If Eve had not taken time to stand and gaze upon the forbidden fruit, perhaps she would have resisted temptation. There was no reason to be looking at it and she accomplished nothing by being there. I will develop my moral character if I ignore temptation and continue with what God has led me to do. However, when we stop and hold conversation with the adversary, we usually end up loosing.

Genesis 19:22,24,25 Haste thee, escape thither; for I cannot do any thing till thou be come thither. Therefore the name of the city was called Zoar. Then the Lord rained upon Sodom and upon Gomorrah brimstone and fire from the Lord out of heaven; And he overthrew those cities and all the plain and all the inhabitants of the cities and that, which grew upon the ground.

There is a statement that the Angel made to Lot (verse 22), and that same statement works in our lives today. Unfortunately, many of our loved ones that are under our umbrella, hang on to Lot's attitude in life without understanding how expensive it is. Nevertheless, notice the angel said, "I cannot do anything till thou be come thither." Nowhere have I found that the wrath of God was poured out on His obedient people. Whether in the days of Noah, Moses, or the children of Israel in Egypt, God did not pour his wrath out on His obedient. However, the disobedient will feel the wrath of God. He chastened every son. Chastening is to learn obedience.

Hebrews 12:6 For whom the Lord loveth he chasteneth and scourgeth every son whom he receiveth.

We need to be able to discern good from evil. Notice that the angel said, "I can not bring judgment upon Sodom until you are out of here." The angel said this not because of Lot or for his sake, but for the sake of Abraham. There are many people who are going to have to learn obedience. They have not learned that yet, and sadly, they will learn by the things that they suffer.

Hebrews 5:8,9 Though he were a Son, yet learned he obedience by the things, which he suffered; And being made perfect, he became the author of eternal salvation unto all them that obey him;

In order for us to be obedient, we must have a servant's heart. It is not our choice, but it is God's will that matters. A servant's heart will let God lead. I will let Him decide, and I will be obedient and follow with a fullness of heart.

Lot portrays the picture in the Book of Revelation that the woman will give birth unto a man-child. The man-child, symbolizing principles, was caught up into the heavens. There are differing opinions about what the woman symbolizes. However, I contend that it is still the body of believers and that the Lord spoke unto John and said, "Let Me show you the things which will come to pass hereafter."

Revelation 1:19 Write the things which thou hast seen and the things which are and the things which shall be hereafter.

Christ's birth is not a future event. It has already happened. I realize that the scripture says the things that are, but also the thing which shall be hereafter. I believe the man-child in Revelation 12 symbolizes the five wise virgins. The woman herself was taken to a place prepared for her, three and a half years.

Revelation 12:1,2,5,6 And there appeared a great wonder in heaven; a woman clothed with the sun, and the moon under her feet and upon her head a crown of twelve stars: And she being with child cried, travailing in birth and pained to be delivered. And she brought forth a man child who was to rule all nations with a rod of iron: and her child was caught up unto God and to his throne. And the woman fled into the wilderness, where she hath a place prepared of God, that they should feed her there a thousand two hundred and threescore days.

Lot had to be out of the city before judgment could come. According to God's standards, he needed to be out.

Genesis 19:27,28,29 And Abraham gat up early in the morning to the place where he stood before the Lord: And he looked toward Sodom and Gomorrah and toward all the land of the plain, and beheld and lo, the smoke of the country went up as smoke of a furnace.

And it came to pass, when God destroyed the cities of the plain, that God remembered Abraham and sent Lot out of the midst of the overthrow, when he overthrew the cities in the which Lot dwelt.

What did this say to you?

God remembered Abraham; it does not say He remembered Lot. He remembered Abraham and pulled Lot out of Sodom. Lot is saved because of Abraham. However, this stopped after the first generation, because of Lot's heart. You have children, grandchildren, friends, and loved ones who are going to be pulled out of the fire. But notice Lot was only pulled out just before the fire hit. He did not get out like Abraham got out, because Abraham never went in.

If you and I raise our children in the world, what chance would they have?

No principles, no morals, no God, no integrity – this is what Lot chose for his children, grandchildren, and his family.

By the time we get to Lot's grandchildren's children, God looked down and said, "None of them can be in My congregation for ten generations." They are the product of sodomy; they are the product of incest. The sins of the parents are visited upon the children (Exodus 20:5).

Lot's eternity – what is it going to be like when he sees this written on the walls of eternity?

He is the culprit and he is the man, but he never had

a servant's heart. Lot is not the great man we hoped he would be. How could he have walked and conversed with Abraham and turned out that sorry? It is a mystery.

How did Demas follow Paul on all his missionary journeys and back slide?

How can people sit in a Pentecostal service where the Holy Ghost and anointing of God are present and not be moved?

They are just not sensitive to eternal matters. How can anyone stay home when the Holy Ghost is going to be meeting His people? The very Spirit of God that is going to take us out of here is going to reward us eternally. The Spirit of God is going to give us our position in the world to come.

Genesis 19:30 And Lot went up out of Zoar and dwelt in the mountain and his two daughters with him; for he feared to dwell in Zoar: and he dwelt in a cave, he and his two daughters.

Lot has gone to the mountain and is confused. Not long ago he argued with the angel to get to Zoar but was miserable there. So he says, "Girls, let's go to the mountain," and they lived in a cave.

Genesis 19:36,37,38 Thus were both the daughters of Lot with child by their father. And the first-born bare a son and called his name Moab: the same is the father of the Moabites unto this day.

And the younger, she also bare a son and called his name Ben-ammi: the same is the father of the children of Ammon unto this day.

Did you ever notice the names of Lot's daughters were never mentioned?

However, their children are named. What we produce will be named throughout eternity. To the sinner all things are sin, and that is the reason that his two daughters were not named. But their children were because the product of incest was a very negative force that had been turned loose upon the earth.

Luke's Gospel tells us that there was "a certain rich man." His name is not mentioned because there is no name to the sinner. He has no identity; he is just a soul in the regions of the damned. But, there was a beggar lying at his gate who had a name, because he was a believer. The rich man's name did not matter. Neither Lot's wife nor his daughters were named. Lot was named because of who Abraham was, and his two grandsons were named because of the evil they did. Nevertheless, in spite of all that evil there is a ray of hope.

Who was the great grandmother of King David and what was her lineage?

Ruth who was a Moabite. She later married Boaz and had a son Obed.

Obed begat Jesse, and Jesse begat David (Matthew 1:5,6).

No matter how sinful or deplorable our people have been, there is hope. If we have it in our hearts to do it, God makes a way.

Abraham & Abimelech

Scripture references:
Genesis 20: 5,7 Said he not unto me, She is my sister? and she, even she herself said, He is my brother: in the integrity of my heart and the innocency of my hands have I done this. Now therefore restore the man his wife; for he is a prophet and he shall pray for thee and thou shall live; and if thou restore her not, know thou that thou shalt surely die, thou and all that are thine.

Genesis 19:37,38	John 6:70 & 17:12
Genesis 20:1,2,3,4,11	Romans 11:29
Daniel 7:25 8:25 11:36	2 Thessalonians 2:3,7

    I thank God for what He has revealed. To Him be the praise and glory forever! This 20th chapter of the Book of Genesis is a unique setting in many ways, and there are some great truths that need to be understood. I will not explain the entire 20th chapter, because I am still seeking revelation on this setting. Therefore let me make the following observation.

    The Lord leaves us with the sovereignty of man. To love, to discipline, and to obtain salvation and all its attributes and integrity are left up to us. We can have integrity or we can drift down the current. Any old dead piece of wood can drift down the current, but it takes people with stamina, integrity, and fortitude to go upstream. The key to our relationship with God is that we demand of ourselves commitment, integrity, and love. These things are within our sphere and jurisdiction. There is no substitute for self-discipline. He that has an ear to hear, let him hear.

Genesis 19:37,38 And the first-born bare a son, and called his name Moab: the same is the father of the Moabites unto this day.

And the younger, she also bares a son and called his name Ben-ammi: the same is the father of the children of Ammon unto this day.

Remember that Lot fled to Zoar. He is a confused dear soul. He thought like many people do today: "If I had more material objects, I would be content and happy." Lot hardly got to Zoar when he said, "I am not content or happy." He said, "Let's go where the angel told us to go in the first place, the mountain." That was one of the better decisions he made.

There is a parallel between Abraham and Lot verses Enoch and Noah.

Now Enoch pleased God and he was raptured. (Hebrews 11) Noah found grace in the eyes of the Lord and he went through the tribulations, he went through the storm. Abraham was a friend of God and he saw the storm from a lofty summit, he saw Sodom and Gomorrah burn, but he was not there. Lot was a believer and he experienced the fire. As he departs from Sodom, being drug by the angel, he depicts to us the woman who flees into the wilderness after the man-child in Revelation 12. Another parallel between Noah and Lot is after the storm they both got drunk. A progressive picture of sin, Noah got drunk and was naked, Lot got drunk, and was the source of two sons by his daughters, and sin brings forth after its kind. Two sons that were born unto Lot by his two daughters lived east of the Dead Sea, so they were geographically located in the path of the Children of Israel, later when they would come, to go into Canaan's land. They had to be tested; therefore, God sees what they are made of.

Selfishness is the basis for all sin. When we are called on to do something for God and His people, our true self is tested.

Who Are the Sons of the Promise?

When Israel, being led by Moses, came into the land of the Moabites, they asked for water, bread, and passage. The Moabites refused. Therefore, they were cursed. None out of either of these tribes will be a part of the children of Israel, or the congregation of the apostles for ten generations.

Now that has much more meaning than we are capable of understanding.

Those in their journey continually test us; they want the bread of life that is in Jesus Christ and the living water. They want to walk with us and they can only walk with us if we love them. Therefore, we are tested, as were Lot's descendents.

- Do people feel relaxed walking with me or do I make them feel uncomfortable?

- Do people feel loved when they are around me?

Love is one commodity that you cannot hide; it radiates out and fills the sphere around us. You know whether I love you or not without me saying a word. Now, I know that the eyes are the mirror of the soul and if you have to make eye contact with me, then I have already messed up. I do not want to labor this point, but I want you to get acquainted with yourself, and I want you to take time to look deeper within yourself. Know yourself and judge yourself and you will not be judged.

Ask yourself, who am I?

This means that I am going to judge myself. If I see something that is not Christ like, I condemn that and say I am not going to serve that. It will not be a part of me and I will seek God until I am sanctified in that matter.

Then I can walk on without it and it will not bring judgment when I face God. There are deeper things that we need to study in our private moments, concerning these great truths and our everyday walk with God.

We can see the message in the origin of these two tribes of people, and how they became an obstacle and hindrance to those in their journey to the promises of God. People in their journey to the promises of God come by us daily, and what we do about that will face us in the eternal world to come.

Genesis 20:1,2,3 And Abraham journeyed from thence toward the south country and dwelled between Kadesh and Shur and sojourned in Gerar. And Abraham said of Sarah his wife, she is my sister: and Abimelech king of Gerar sent and took Sarah. But God came to Abimelech in a dream by night and said to him, Behold thou art but a dead man, for the woman which thou hast taken; for she is a man's wife.

After this, Abraham journeys south. Allow me to lay a little bit of foundation here. In the Book of Daniel, chapters 7,8,9,10,11, you will study the coming, the origin, and the product of the anti-Christ. In Daniel 11, you will find that the anti-Christ will come out of the old Syrian Empire. When Alexander the Great died at about 31 years old with venereal disease, he had no sons to take his place. His empire was divided among his four generals. Egypt is referred to as the nation of the south. Assyria is referred to as king of the north, and north of Jerusalem is Assyria. Egypt and Turkey went to one of the generals, and so it was divided among the four.

We are coming to the place where the great controversy takes place, and out of Assyria will come the anti-Christ. At that time, there was Syria and Assyria. Assyria, in that hour, took in Iran, Iraq, and down to Kuwait. All this was the old Assyrian Empire; the king of the North ruled this. Out of the region near the Tigris-Euphrates River, Babylon, Iraq, Iran, and Assyria, the anti-Christ will come, according to Daniel. So we are going to be watching closely. Iraq, Iran, and Assyria will come together as one nation. There will be a man of peace from this region; he is the man we will watch closely.

I call your attention to Thessalonians where we are told, he who letteth will let until he will be taken out and then the man of sin will be revealed.

2 Thessalonians 2:3,7 Let no man deceive you by any means for that day shall not come, except there come a falling away first and that man of sin be revealed, the son of perdition; For the mystery of iniquity doth already work: only he who now letteth will let, until he be taken out of the way.

References for son of perdition:

John 6:70 & 17:12

Reference for anti-Christ:

Daniel 7:25 & 8:25 & 11:36

He that is holding back will hold back until he is taken out, and then the man of sin will be revealed. This could happen any time.

I will use this illustration. If the anti-Christ is trying to come through our door and the God-fearing, heaven-born, saints of God are on the other side holding that door shut, we are keeping the anti-Christ in check.

It is not the armies of the world; it is God-fearing people who believe in Jesus Christ. When the God-fearing people of this world, the ones holding the door shut, are taken, then the anti-Christ can open the door, walk in, and be revealed.

So, how close are we?

We are looking for him now!

We are looking for the Christ, but the world is going to find the anti-Christ!

Abraham moves to the south, traveling to where the king of the Philistines lives. His camp is outside the city, but he and his people find the city of the Philistines.

What is the Bible definition symbolizing sin and flesh?

Nations. Egypt is one of them. The Philistine always symbolizes flesh or sin in the flesh. Another nation is the Jebusites. They were controlling the area where the temple was to be built. They have a prophetic word and picture of their own. Abraham has moved down to the capitol of the Philistines. This is a tribulation scene; you will also realize that God is a God of another chance. Abraham tells the very same lie in the 20th chapter that he told in the 12th chapter. The very same reason he lied in the 20th chapter is the same reason he lied in the 12th chapter.

There is a parallel between chapters 12 and 20. Both chapters include places that depict sin.

Sin influences and affects us all, our environment, our associates, and even the things we do. In the 12th chapter, Abraham lied in Egypt..

Now we are in the promise land. Abraham travels to the capitol, Gerar, (House of the Kings), where the Philistines King lived. Geographically, in New Testament times this was in the region of Joppa. I refer to Joppa, as hells half-acre. It was at Joppa where God gave Peter the vision of the sheet with the unclean animals that brought him back up to Caesarea, where he brought that great message to Cornelius the centurion of the Italian band.

(For Peter's vision, see Acts 10:9-16.)

The land of the Philistines (the land of the flesh) was from Joppa, from five to seven miles wide, going down the coastline and down to the point, crossing into Egypt. All of it has a prophetic word. The Philistines gave God's people fits through the years. God would use them to chastise Israel, when Israel would become Idolaters. You can go right out of the Philistines land into sin itself, right into Egypt. Although Abraham was in the promise land, he went back because the king of the flesh influenced him.

And what is man's first instinct?

Survival.

Abraham at 99 years old is still worried about his 89-year-old wife. He is in the wrong place and being influenced by those around him. In the Bible for the first time, the word prophet is used. I am bewildered at this event; Abraham has been influenced and drawn in. He has forgotten his identity. He has willingly and willfully falsified a relationship between him and the Church (Sarah). Not only did Abraham say Sarah was his sister, but Sarah said he was her brother.

Genesis 20:4,5,7 But Abimelech had not come near her: and he said Lord, wilt thou slay also a righteous nation? Said he not unto me, She is my sister? And she, even she herself said, He is my brother: in the integrity of my heart and innocency of my hands have I done this. Now therefore restore the man his wife; for he is a prophet, and he shall pray for thee, and thou shalt live: and if thou restore her not, know thou that thou surely die, thou and all that are thine.

This is a prophetic word. There is something going on that we do not see. Something is going to transpire in the Church in the last days that is going to parallel with this 20th chapter. This is not a normal setting; this is not a natural thing. God knew Abraham had lied and failed. He knew Abraham had encouraged the Church to lie. Yet when Abimelech took Sarah into his domain, God proclaimed, "You are a dead man!" Abraham excused himself for doing it by saying, "God is nowhere around here."

Genesis 20:11 And Abraham said, because I thought, surely the fear of God is not in this place; and they will slay me for my wife's sake.

Abimelech is not a name, but a title, like king or president. The word appears later in the scripture but is referring to a different man. Have you ever been somewhere and thought the Lord is nowhere in this place? Abraham made an error, thinking God is not here. The true test of a man's character is what he does when no one seems to be watching.

Abraham told Sarah, "God is not in Philistine country, or here in hell's half-acre. Just tell him I am your brother." But God was there!

The pneuma breath of God is in every individual, and the soul within that individual wants to be related again to the Father, God. God is the God of another chance. Abraham concluded t He was not there, and did what he wanted. God came to Abimelech and told him Abraham was a prophet.

Romans 11:29 For the gifts and callings of God are without repentance.

God has called you and me. The work and the plan for our lives will not change. It is a providential act of God, and God has called every one of us. The first thing that God has called us to do is fear God, keep His commandments, and love one another.

One of the greatest tasks we face is to remember not to make the mistakes that Abraham did. God is here. What we choose to do and say is going to affect our eternity and the eternity of others. When God spoke with Abimelech, knowing Abraham had lied, God told him, "He is a prophet." God did not see Abraham as a man who lied. He saw Abraham as His Prophet.

Abraham- Father of the Promise

Scripture references:
Genesis 21:3,6,8,9 And Abraham called the name of his son that was born unto him, whom Sarah bare to him, Isaac. And Sarah said, God hath made me laugh, so that all that hear, will laugh with me. And the child grew and was weaned: and Abraham made a great feast the same day that Isaac was weaned. And Sarah saw the son of Hagar, the Egyptian, which she had born unto Abraham, mocking.

Genesis 21:1,2,10,11,14　　John 14:26,27
Deuteronomy 16:16　　　　Hebrews 5:8,9

    I pray that God would give us the opportunity to look into the depth of what is transpiring in the Book of Genesis. There are many prophetic overtones in this foundational structure of Abraham. Hurriedly, we will recognize that Abraham is one of those great patriarchs that has given unto us an act of obedience that has brought him into an eternal covenant. Through his obedience to God, Abraham has shown us the first foundation stone and some of its great benefits. I have studied this somewhat and I cannot find anything that gives Abraham the role that he was living out, other than his obedience to God. God called on him to do some very great things, and because he obeyed, he became the great father of promise! His descendents became the sons of the promise! They were the sons of the promise when they obeyed. God did whatever He needed to do to bring those in line of obedience. Abraham never one time said, "God do not, do that." We as the Church need to learn obedience as well.

Genesis 21:1,2,3 And the Lord visited Sarah as he had said, and the Lord did unto Sarah as he had spoken. For

Sarah conceived and bare Abraham a son in his old age, at the set time of which God had spoken to him. And Abraham called the name of his son that was born unto him, Whom Sarah bare to him, Isaac.

The Lord came but we do not know in what form. Some theologians think it was Christ himself, some think it was an angelical visitation, I do not know. All I know is that He came and made a statement, confirming the fact, that within a year, Sarah would have a son by Abraham.

There is a great deal of prophetic involvement here because Sarah plays the part of the Church and the man-child symbolizes the principles.

There is a deficiency of the principles of God in the Church world today. However, I assure you before this is all over, there will be principles back in the Church. We are living in an hour where nothing is quite right or wrong. There are no blacks and there are no whites in sin and righteousness. The Lord told us the Church will have principles. The Church is going to birth it; we will have a burden on our hearts from God. We will receive a visitation from above and come back to the place where the world does not matter. We have fads and fashion, traditions. Grandma did it, and grandpa did it, and mom does it. Alcoholics grow alcoholics, and people who are not obedient and faithful to church raise children who are not obedient and faithful to church. We hand these genes and behaviors on from generation to generation, but it will change. The tribulation will be an evangelist of its own kind, and this is a sad commentary.

Sarah had prayed for so long that she had given up. Some things are miracles and some things are healings. Healing is a progressive thing and a miracle is instantaneous. Many times we say, "God please heal this person," and all the time we want a miracle. We are asking one thing and expecting another. Healing is a progressive thing. For example, you cut your hand, next day it is sore, and the third day it is so sore that you cannot stand it, but there is a healing already starting. We want a miracle and we ask for healing. It is the same way in our prayer life concerning people. Many times we come to the Lord, asking for something and we forget whom we are praying for is a free moral agent. We want God to take their free moral agency away from them until they are old enough or able to handle it. However God will not do that. He can get you by the ear, nose, or pull your arm, rearrange the furniture in your life, even to the point of death to get you where you need to be, but you are still a free moral agent. When two agree together for someone to get saved, that focuses the eyes of God right on that individual. God begins to move in their free moral agency, and God begins to move the furniture around. Bad things start happening and physical things are happening, and the first thing you know we are hollering, "God heal my child!" Nevertheless, all the time we are asking God to save them. This nullifies our faith and prayer. When we ask God to save someone's soul at any cost, just remember there is a cost, because that individual is not going to by nature turn to God.

Therefore, Sarah is going to have a son and she laughed. There are two laughing in this lesson today – Sarah and Ishmael. Sarah is laughing with God about her having a son. She is excited about her son. Ishmael laughs, but his laugh has a very different meaning, origin, purpose, and motive. Sarah laughs and bears Isaac, Ishmael laughs and is kicked out of the camp. We must understand the motive and what is coming forth in our expression.

Sarah bears a son and they call him "laughter." She says, "Abraham here is laughter." Of course, at 100 years old, he could laugh.

Genesis 21:4 And Abraham circumcised his son Isaac being eight days old, as God had commanded him.

God commanded Abraham to be perfect, walk upright before Him, and keep the covenant of circumcision.

They were not called upon prior to this to be perfect; circumcision has to do with the flesh. The Arab nation today circumcises their males at 13 years old, because that is how old Ishmael was when God gave Abraham the covenant and Abraham circumcised Ishmael. It was on the eighth day that they brought Jesus into the temple and circumcised Him. While Joseph and Mary were bringing him into the temple, they met Simeon and Anna. What a great day that was.

Why the eighth day?

Why specifically did God say the eighth day?

The eighth day is the era of new commitment.

There were three high and holy feast days in Israel. There were others, but there were three major ones where every male had to appear before the Lord.

Deuteronomy 16:16 Three times in a year shall thy males appear before the Lord thy God in the place which he shall choose; in the feast of unleavened bread and in the feast of weeks and in the feast of tabernacles: and they shall not appear before the Lord empty:

• Feast of Unleavened Bread Passover:

We know about Egypt and the Passover origin. It was the source of giving life.

• Feast of Weeks, Pentecost:

50 days later actually, Pentecost was the eighth day! God said we would have a week of weeks.

That goes over into the hour that were also living and it is the days of Israel's troubles, a week of weeks, and the eighth day there after.

- Feast of the Tabernacle:

This festival was observed to commemorate the wandering of Israel in the wilderness. It is sometimes called the feast of booths also.

Seven times seven equals 49, and on the next day, on the eighth day, God gave Moses the law on Sinai on the 50th day. He has a new nation without government. They have come out of 400 years of bondage and now they are a nation without guidelines or structure. All they knew was bondage.

We have Pentecost on the front of our church because we came out of sin and darkness and into the family of God. The Ten Commandments led the children of Israel across the wilderness as the Holy Ghost will lead us until we get home. We are a new people. We need something to guide our lives, conversations, and conduct. God gave Moses everything on the mountain. The Holy Ghost touches every phase of our lives. When they crucified our Lord and Savior it was on Passover. A week of weeks, which would be forty nine days, and the fiftieth day which is the eighth day after seven times seven (or perfection times perfection or completion times completion). The eighth day was a new beginning. It was a covenant under a new era. It was a new beginning.

Circumcision is sanctification. It is sanctifying the vessel, the heart, the flesh. It is the flesh that gets us in trouble. The law was weak in the flesh, and because of that, God sent his only Son in the likeness of sinful flesh. When Jesus was crucified, nails were driven in his hands, feet, and a crown of thorns placed on his head. Sanctification, Peter says, is the circumcision of the heart.

God made a new covenant with Abraham. This new covenant made Abraham the father of the sons of promise. Never before had they been called on to deal with the flesh, never before had they been called on to circumcise. Therefore, on the eighth day, Abraham circumcised Isaac,

Who Are the Sons of the Promise?

and now Jews circumcise their sons on the eighth day. Isaac is the son of the promise, as long as Isaac obeys God. Isaac is a unique man; we will be talking about him in the future. He is a type of the Christian and there was no fight in Isaac. People today who fight need a rebirth. Isaac symbolizes Jesus Christ. The inheritance came through Isaac. Without Isaac, there is no fulfillment of Promise. So it is without Jesus Christ – there is no inheritance and no tomorrow. Without the shed blood of Jesus, there is no remission of sin.

Was Isaac ever in a fighting situation?

Was Isaac ever in rebellion?

Isaac told the same lie his daddy did, but he also had consequences. Isaac was that unique fellow who was sandwiched between Abraham, the obedient, and Jacob, the disobedient. Abraham was the father of the promise, and Jacob was a fellow that would not line up with the promise. Isaac was a man in between. This man who was the first son of the promise made obedience his lifestyle. He remained obedient to his father, and like Abraham, desired to submit to God.

Genesis 21:8 And the child grew and was weaned: and Abraham made a great feast the same day that Isaac was weaned.

Isaac was three years old and Abraham 103 years. That was a great day in the life of a man, when a son lived through those first three years. Now he is weaned and will take on the nourishment that will develop him into manhood. However, while they were having their high and holy day celebrating Isaac, notice what this Arabian ass did!

Genesis 21:9,10,11 And Sarah saw the son of Hagar the Egyptian, which she had born unto Abraham, mocking.

Wherefore she said unto Abraham, Cast out this bondwoman and her son: for the son of this bondwoman shall not be heir with my son, even with Isaac. And the thing was very grievous in Abraham's sight because of his son.

Sarah laughed and Ishmael laughed.

Now there was a great deal of jealously and conflict from this time forward. Nevertheless, up to this time, there was a common consent that Hagar's son Ishmael was Sarah's son. Sarah and Hagar had more trouble when Sarah birthed Isaac. Abraham, Sarah, and Hagar thought that Ishmael was the promised son, though he was not. Isaac is the son of promise, by Abraham and Sarah.

The Church (Sarah) has accepted the half-breed, (½ worldly, ½ Christian) Church descendents.

• We have accepted them as being those that are going to inherit the rapture, heaven, and the streets of gold. They are going to inherit everything that the Father has, for all that is His is ours.

• We have accepted the half-breeds, we have come to believe they are our descendents and this is where God's hand is resting.

Because we have not seen principles birthed yet, do not give up on God. Ephesians said that He has given us apostles, prophets, evangelists, pastors and teachers for the perfecting of the saints and for the edifying the body of Christ until we come into the full measure and statute of Jesus. The gifts of the Holy Ghost were given to us to bring us into the fullness of Christ. Ishmael is not the fullness of Christ; he is not that man. Some say we are there. We do not love right yet, we allow situations to reduce us to our lower nature.

Sarah, Abraham, and Hagar accepted the apostasy as

being the true inherited son of God. The principles of God were then introduced to the Church, but the Church said, "No, this half-breed will not receive the inheritance." In other words, Sarah woke up and the Church will wake up. Do not get upset with Sarah. Remember it grieved Abraham, and he came back to God and said, "what about my son Ishmael?" God told Abraham to listen to Sarah. She has been living a life without the faith, but now has the product. Follow her; follow the Church. She has awakened. If Sarah would have had faith, (that God was going to give her a son), there would have been no role reversal, but Sarah had lost her faith. Sarah tells Hagar to leave and take this young man, Ishmael (now age 17). He is not going to be part of the inheritance. Then war came to the camp and has never left. War is in the camp today, and will stay in the camp between the Arabs and the Jews until this thing is over. Because the Jews have not accepted Christ, they do not have His support in all the conflict they are going through. The peacemaker is not there.

What did we inherit from Jesus?

His shed blood and forgiveness of our sins. He also gave us His peace for He said, "My peace I leave with you." Who left the Jews peace? They do not accept the Peace-giver, so they have no peace. The Arabs have no peace and Israel will not have peace. Even though they sign treaties, they will not have peace until the Peace-giver is accepted. Jesus said, "My peace I leave with you."

John 14:27 Peace I leave with you, my peace I give you unto you: not as the world giveth, give I unto you. Let not your heart be troubled, neither let it be afraid.

So, when the enemy comes and tries to get us out of sorts, remember we have inherited peace from Jesus Christ.

What is the promise of the Father?

The Holy Ghost is the promise of the Father; peace is the promise of Christ.

John 14:26 But the comforter, which is the Holy Ghost whom the Father will send in my name, he will teach you all things and bring all things to your remembrance, whatsoever I have said to you.

People who have not received that promise still have a void in their lives. When we do not make Him an honored guest in our everyday life, it creates a void in us. Many people speak in tongues but do not have the promise of the Father.

Genesis 21:14 And Abraham rose up early in the morning and took bread and a bottle of water and gave it unto Hagar, putting it on her shoulder and the child and sent her away: and she departed and wandered in the wilderness of Beer-sheba.

Abraham gave Hagar a bottle of water and bread and sent her into what is now the land of the Arabs.

The Arabians have the region from the Red Sea to the edge of the Mediterranean Sea to the Euphrates River. That is where Ishmael went and that is where Ishmael lives. The battle fields are being established between the Arabs and the Jews in these distant hours of Abraham, Sarah, Hagar, Ishmael, and Isaac. We have a domestic problem that has been there and will remain there, because the Jews will not accept Christ and the Arabs are half-breeds. You can only expect war from a situation like that.

We need not be bewildered about the Middle East and its problems. All the players are on the stage for the first time and their descendents will remain until the end of time.

Genesis 21:25,27,28,30,31 And Abraham reproved Abimelech because of a well of water, which Abimelech's servants had violently taken away. And Abraham took sheep and oxen and gave them unto Abimelech; and both of them made a covenant. And Abraham set seven ewe lambs of the flock by themselves. And he said," For these seven ewe lambs shalt thou take of my hand, that they may be a witness unto me, that I have digged this well. Wherefore he called that place Beer-sheba: because there they sware both of them.

Abraham remained in the area of Bersheba. "Ber" translates as "a well that has been dug." If it were an artesian well, it would have a different name. In some places, it is called "a well of oath" and sometimes called "the oath of seven." It was here that Abraham met King Abimelech, who was the king of the Philistine cities. Here is the flesh again.

Abraham has come to the place where he is drawing the line in the sand. Abimelech (the flesh) has come to take the well in Bersheba. Abraham refused to give Abimelech the well. It was about 12 feet across and went through 16 foot of rock. (This is dealing with our relationship to the well of living water; we cannot sacrifice salvation and give it to the flesh, the adversary.)

When Abraham and Abimelech were standing at the well of Bersheba, Abraham brought seven female lambs and gave them to Abimelech. Then Abraham stated to Abimelech, "This is a covenant between you and me. This well is mine and it will always be mine."

Why the female lambs?

The female lambs represent future generations. They represent productivity. If a ram had been sacrificed, then the covenant would stop when he died. As long as the

Church is giving life, it keeps her from the Philistines. Our children will continue to receive life and the covenant that we make will continue to be their covenant.

The relationship that we made with God will not be intermingled with this last hour deception that we see taking its place in the church world today.

In addition, this covenant was a lasting covenant between Abraham and Abimelech. As Abraham was then, we are now in the line of providence; the events in the Middle East are the last few grains of sand falling through the hourglass of God.

So be sure to keep your name inscribed in the Book of Life and ready to go when the trumpet of God sounds.

Abraham's Covenant of Covenants

Scripture references:
Genesis 17:6 & 18:18
And I will make thee exceeding fruitful and I will make nations of thee and kings shall come out of thee.
Seeing that Abraham shall surely become a great and mighty nation, and all the nations of the earth shall be blessed in him.

Job 1:8	Romans 10:14,15,17
Ecclesiastes 1:4	Hebrews 11:6 & 12:1
John 3:29	Revelation 3:12 & 5:9,10
Acts 8:30,31	Revelation 21:1,7

Isaac depicts Christ, but the events in his life, his personality, his position, his labor follows this line, and he symbolizes the Son of The Promise! The Lord confirmed His covenant to Abraham through Isaac, and the inheritance continued through Isaac. Therefore, without Isaac there is no fulfillment of promise!

Without Jesus Christ, there is no eternal inheritance and no tomorrow. There is nothing without Him. Without the shed blood of Jesus, there is no forgiveness of sin.

In the circumcision, there was a covenant. Remember the circumcision was the covenant of covenants.

In this lesson, we want you to see the natural covenant paralleled in the spiritual sense. It is God's intention to bring the covenant to its fullest capacity in your life and mine. So here we have thirteen things that God promised Abraham. We say that we are sons of the promise, so let's see what He is saying to us.

Thirteen things that God promised Abraham hinge on faith and obedience. The covenant was broken with disobedience. We must have faith to believe God is a reality in our life.

Hebrews 11:6 For without faith it is impossible to please him: for him that cometh to God must believe that he is and he is a rewarder of them that diligently seek him.

God promised there will be a great number of benefits when we have faith in the promise and God, but our doubts can nullify it. When the covenant was made with Abraham, it was established, fortified, and enlarged. Each time we read one of the scriptures from Genesis 12,13, 15, 17, or 22, God is requiring a little more and giving more.

Just as it was to the seven Churches of Asia, each time we step into the next church, God requires more and promises more. The thief on the cross received salvation, but that is it. There are thirty-fold, sixty-fold, and ninety-fold Christians. We will find ourselves in eternity somewhere between the one-fold Christian and the hundred-fold Christian, but we must be faithful and obedient to the end.

How can we have faith except there be a preacher or teacher?

Romans 10:14,15,17 How then shall they call on him in whom they have not believed? and how shall they believe in him whom they have not heard and how shall they hear without a preacher? And how shall they preach, except they are sent? (In-part) So then faith cometh by hearing and hearing by the word of God.

What this is saying to me?

Acts 8:30,31 And Philip ran thither to him and heard him

read the prophet Isaiah and said, understand what thou readest? And he said, how can I except some man should guide me? And he desired Philip that he would come up and sit with him.

My job is to teach you. After you're taught, stand on the Word of God and be obedient. That will enrich you.

For clarification, the first five Churches in the Book of Revelation are never given any promise that has to do above the earth's surface. It does not give any promises in the eternal heavens; it is all earthly. However, when God gets to the Church of Philadelphia, He requires more. We are moving up the ladder, from 10-30-60-90-100 fold, and with each Church He is requiring more. The Philadelphia Church has more light so more is required, but he that overcometh shall become a pillar in the temple of God.

Revelation 3:12 (In-part) Him that overcometh will I make a pillar in the temple of my God and he shall go no more out:

And to the Laodicean Church, He says, "I challenge you to buy gold tried in the fire (that is total purity). If you will do that, you will sit with Me on My Father's throne." He does not offer that to any other church. We have the light and if our attitudes are right, faithful, and committed, we can be the kings and priests in the world to come. God gave Abraham a great position. God also gave John the Baptist a great position, but you and I can excel.

John 3:29 He that hath the bride is the bridegroom: but the friend of the bridegroom, which standeth and heareth him, rejoiceth greatly because of the bridegroom's voice: this is my joy therefore is fulfilled.

John the Baptist said, "I will be a friend unto the

groom, and in the voice of the groom shall my joy be fulfilled." I will be a groomsman, but I will not be a part of the Bride of Christ. That is the highest John the Baptist can go, because he had nothing to do with receiving the Holy Ghost; he did not have a choice.

When we receive the baptism of the Holy Ghost, we follow and serve with integrity, commitment, determination, and faith. It is our choice. We have a greater light and God requires more from us.

Abraham would not qualify to serve on our deacon board. He was the father of twilight and did not have all the light. Noah would not qualify to serve as a leader in the church, he was serving to a distant light, but we walk in the light. Noah's boys found him naked and drunk. We have a greater light; more is required of us, and the promises that God gave to Abraham were earthly.

I. Abraham's name shall be great!

Those that are instrumental in winning souls will be given crowns in the world to come, and friend your name will be great. Can you imagine how thankful you will be when we get home eternally and find that one individual that was instrumental in pointing us to Jesus Christ? Outside of Christ, they will be the greatest name in Heaven and given a crown because they pointed us to Jesus Christ. The name will be great, not as the world sees it, but as God sees it. It is deplorable whom the world looks to as great; most are a reproach to the nation. However, with our covenant, God says our name will be great in the eternal world.

II. A great nation shall come from him!

We are pilgrims and strangers here, we are sojourners, we are not citizens of this earth but citizens of the world to come. We have a following there. We have a nation there of the lives that we prayed and agreed for their salvation. We have worked, loved, tutored, taught, and led them. Let your name be mentioned in another city or town and your commitment to God is what is brought to mind. How is it going to be in that world to come, with all of your loved ones already in the cathedral in the sky, watching you, when your name is mentioned?

Hebrews 12:1 Wherefore seeing we also are compassed about with so great a cloud of witnesses, let us lay aside every weight and the sin which doth so easily beset us and let us run with patience the race that is set before us.

When the sons of God came together in Heaven and Job's name was mentioned, this is what the Lord said:

Job 1:8 Hast thou considered my servant Job, that there is none like him in the earth, a perfect and an upright man, one that feareth God, and escheweth evil?

Out of your life, integrity, commitment, and your love, they will become a great number, a great nation, and a great people, because we are committed to our covenant with God.

III. He should be a blessing so great that in him all the families of the earth are blessed!

You are a great blessing. Can you imagine how proud your loved ones who are in Heaven watching you this morning are of you?

It is the covenant people that move heaven. The people who have faith and are committed are the people who the adversary tries to accuse. Though he is accusing you and me in the courtroom of God, God knows the truth and only the truth stands before Him. You are a blessing in this world, and you will be a blessing in the world to come. Because of Abraham, and God's covenant with him, all the families of the earth will be blessed.

IV. To him personally, to thee, and to his seed, should he give Palestine forever to inherit!

Revelation 5:10 And hast made us unto our God kings and priests: and we shall reign on the earth.

This is the four beasts and the twenty-four elders. I call this the Philadelphia and the Laodicean order of overcomers. Revelation 5 tells us exactly who these four beasts and twenty-four elders are.

Revelation 5:9 And they sung a new song, saying Thou art worthy to take the book and to open the seals thereof: for thou wast slain and hast redeemed us to God by thy blood out of every kindred and tongue and people and nation;

This is the entire picture of the redeemed, the Philadelphia and Laodicean order of the redeemed. We are redeemed out of every nation, kindred, tongue, and people. Jesus not only redeemed us, but He also made us kings and priests, and we shall rule on the earth!

Ecclesiastes 1:4 One generation passeth away and another generation cometh: but the earth abideth forever.

Revelation 21:1 And I saw a new heaven and a new earth: for the first heaven and the first earth passed away; and there was no more sea.

In addition, all those fertile valleys that make up the ocean floor right now will be like the Garden of Eden in the world to come.

This earth will be purified by fire, and we, the higher order of God, will rule right here on this earth. He uses two scenarios because we are under one of two orders. We are either kings or priests.

Kings rule people, kingdoms, and government. Priests are the spiritual order, and in the world to come, there will be both. Because this world will be renovated, only the godly will persevere, rule, and reign on the earth.

When Jesus handed out talents and pounds, he told them to take them. One man took his one and gained ten. Jesus said he would rule ten cities. The next man took his talent and gained five. Jesus told him he would rule five cities. This is not in Heaven but here on this earth, the new earth, the earth that will abide forever. The earth was never a mistake, but made in perfection – the perfect amount of oxygen, temperature, plants – a balance that could only be created, not a random molecular collision.

Not all of us will be kings and priests; it's about faith and obedience. The covenant that God made with Abraham has been replaced with a new covenant – a new covenant with the house of Israel and God's people. God will be their God and they will be His people. God has given us, through Jesus Christ, a better covenant.

As Gentiles, we are grafted in. We represent that wild olive branch and it is a great responsibility. When God laid out his law in Leviticus (Leviticus means "law"), He instructs Israel to be a nation of priests. They refused God's commandment and created a law stating Jews cannot speak to Samaritans. Therefore, God said, "I cannot use you. I will go to the Gentiles to be My priestly nation." In other words, we are to evangelize the world. God has made us a priestly people. If we do what Israel did and turn down the opportunity and obligation to be a priestly people, then God will turn to someone else.

Talents and church service

He is speaking to us; this is part of the covenant. In addition, there is an inheritance for us, for all of eternity, an inheritance for us and our seed forever and ever.

V. The multitude of his seed should be as the dust of

the earth!

How many people can you influence, touch, and see saved now? When you drop a dollar or ten dollars in the missions bucket, we do not have a clue how far that goes. Those people who give themselves through supporting, building, giving their time, labor, and finances to being a part of the kingdom of God...we will never know how far reaching that is until we get to eternity. We are selfish people, I am selfish because I want as great of an eternity as I possibly can, so I do all I can for Him now. I am not doing it for you or the church. It will bless you, but I am doing it for God, and God will reward us through out the ceaseless ages of eternity.

How many people will you and I reach while we are here?

How far reaching can this church be?

Only God knows that answer...

Remember it is faith and obedience that will bring us into that relationship where we are the sons of the promise!

Israel lost the promises of the covenant because they refused to walk by faith in obedience to God, then we were brought in, the Gentiles.

I will list the remainder of the 13 and not expound on them further since they are self-explanatory. Remember these are parallel to the covenant of old (flesh) and our new covenant (spiritual) with Jesus Christ...

VI. That whoever blessed him will be blessed and whosoever cursed him will be cursed.

VII. He should be the father of many nations.

VIII. Kings should proceed from Him.

IX. *The covenant shall be perpetual, "an everlasting Covenant."*

X. *God will be a God to him and his seed.*

XI. *The land of Canaan shall be "an everlasting possession."*

XII. *His seed shall possess the gate of his enemies.*

XIII. *In his seed shall the nations of the earth be blessed.*

The covenant made with Abraham is in Genesis 12:1,2,3. It is confirmed and enlarged to him in Genesis 12:6,7; 13:14-17; 15:1-21; 17:1-14; and 22:15-18.

Therefore, I leave you with this…

Revelation 21:7 He that overcometh shall inherit all things; and I will be his God and he shall be my son…

Three Days Journey

Scripture references:
Genesis 22:1,2 And it came to pass after these things, that God did tempt Abraham and said unto him, Abraham: and said unto him, Abraham: and he said, Behold, here I am. And he said, Take now thy son, thine only son Isaac, whom thou lovest and get thee unto the land of Moriah; and offer him there for a burnt offering upon one of the mountains which I will tell thee of.

Genesis 22:1,3,4,5,6,7,8	2 Timothy 3:16
Matthew 28:20	Hebrews 5:14 6:1
Romans 8:35	James 1:13

How many books in the New Testament do not refer back to Abraham? Very few – they all come back to Abraham, because this is the foundation of a covenant that will take us beyond life. The greater your commitment to God and the greater your integrity to God, the greater you will serve in the world to come. The challenges that you and I go through today will prepare us here to serve him there on an eternal scale. I believe that in this life today, we are only preparing ourselves to serve

God on an eternal scale. Look at life; about the time you learn how to do something, you move into another dimension. About the time, you learn how to be a parent, you are too old to be a parent. Life is a learning process, getting us ready for tomorrow and the world to come.

Abraham has now successfully either repented or fulfilled the requirement of God. He did miss it a few times, and he is not without mistakes. However, neither are you and I.

Who Are the Sons of the Promise?

Abraham is ready for the next step; this will be a great step. He is ready to prove his love to God. The only instrument that I know for a calibration of love is service and commitment. The only way that I can prove to you that I love you is what I am willing to sacrifice.

Abraham is ready to move from the scene of Isaac and Ishmael. What God said to Abraham about Ishmael was never debated. Abraham accepted God's Word. God told Abraham in the 22nd chapter to offer his son, the one he loved more than anything. God said, "Bring him to Mount Moriah, build an altar, and sacrifice him to Me."

Genesis 22:2 And he said, "Take now thy son, thine only son Isaac, whom thou lovest and get thee into the land of Moriah; and offer him there for a burnt offering upon one of the mountains which I will tell thee of.

The Lord is referring to Abraham's only son Isaac. We know that Abraham has another son, but thine only son is symbolic of Jesus Christ, the only begotten son. We must remember that Jesus is the only begotten son. He sits next to his Father and holds a position of authority over us.

Isaac was between 18 and 25 years old at this time. He was born in 1897 B.C. After researching, I believe this occurred around 1872 B.C.

When would that have happened in his life? At what age?

At the age of thirty, the Hebrew men were considered men. He had to be younger than thirty, because the focus is still on Abraham's obedience. God knew Abraham loved Ishmael and Isaac. He loved both boys and begged with God concerning Ishmael. God said a nation would come out of Ishmael.

Can you Imagine what all went on in Abraham's tent?

What do you think Sarah did, when Abraham told her what he was about to do?

I can only imagine…the thing Abraham is about to do is big… super big! There is no specific scripture about Sarah knowing that Abraham planned to offer Isaac as a sacrifice, but he would be gone for a week. I believe Abraham was not doing this without Sarah knowing it, and it appears she supported Abraham's decision.

Abraham did not know that Mt. Moriah was the very same mountain that God was going to offer His Son Jesus. He was just following God's word. Zion is a part of that region of the mountains of Moriah. God told Abraham that he would tell him which mountain. You and I are called on to make particular commitments and sacrifices that maybe someone else is not going to have to make. Abraham had to travel from Beer-Sheba and go north to the east and he was going to go to Salem.

Jews rule Salem – Jerusalem.

He is coming to the mountains at Jerusalem. It's about a forty to fifty mile journey, and it takes him three days to reach the mountain. That is three measures of time. Three experiences will bring us from our tents of habitation, to our mountains of obedience.

Salvation is departing from the tent. Sanctification is separating from the tent. The Holy Ghost is the strength to climb the mountain.

There is three days journey from where you and I got saved to where God really wants us to be in our obedience to God.

Three days journey from Abraham's tent to Mt. Moriah…

That first day was salvation, the second day was sanctification, and that third day was going to take the

Holy Ghost and only the Holy Ghost to offer that son.

In addition, our journey is that way; we can only go so far in salvation. Salvation gives us eternal life, but for us to take that next step with God we must be sanctified. Then for us to scale that mountain, it is going to take a lot of God and the leadership of the Holy Ghost. It is going to take strength that we do not have. Bear in mind that if Isaac is around 25 years old, then Abraham is going to climb this mountain and he is 125 years old. Hell was saying, "I do not believe the old man can make it."

When you and I look at the challenge that God has put before us, hell tells you that you cannot make it. The flesh tells you that you cannot make it. God has called on all of us. We all have gifts and callings, and our gifts and callings are going to serve us and serve ours through the world to come. We are going to have to make up our minds that we are going to make it and to do what God has called me to do. It does not matter if Peter or John does not want to do it; I am going to do it.

How are we going to make it?

Through the leadership of the Holy Ghost, our faith, and our obedience, our love for God and our love for one another. That is how we are going to make it.

Genesis 22:1 And it came to pass after these things that God did tempt Abraham and said unto him, Abraham: and he said Behold, here I am.

James 1:13 Let no man say when he is tempted, I am tempted of God: for God cannot be tempted with evil, neither tempteth he any man.

Now I do not know just for sure what all incorporated these things. We know that Abraham has made a covenant with Abimelech. We see here that the Lord is making the observation that after these things, God tempts Abraham. God tempts no man; this is a step of obedience. Abraham is being proved and tested. Abraham tested in two great fields – one is faith and the other is obedience. These things, faith and obedience are also tested in our lives. Salvation gives us eternal life, but then we are tested and that puts us in Canaan land figuratively speaking. However, where about on the scale are we going to serve eternally? The only way God can determine that is how we serve him with faith and obedience, here and now, through testing.

Genesis 22:3 And Abraham rose up early in the morning and saddled his ass and took two of his young men with him and Isaac his son and clave the wood for the burnt offering and rose up and went unto the place of which God had told him.

Abraham did not say, "Let us wait for a more convenient hour." He rose up early in the morning in obedience to God, and headed out.

<u>This was a whole burnt offering:</u>

Not atonement. Isaac could never become the atonement. Only one can be the atonement and that is Jesus Christ. If it was the atonement itself – and it is good that you understand this – it would not be a whole burnt offering, because they would catch the blood of the ox, the lamb, the pigeon, or the turtledove, and would offer that blood according to your financial status for sin atonement. Therefore, we understand that Isaac is taking the position, depicting, and foretelling the death of Christ, but God was exact in his statement. He wants a burnt offering – a whole burnt offering! Had it been a paschal lamb offering, other things would have been involved. Since it is a whole burnt offering, we are not going to catch his blood. All you need is an altar, wood, a knife and the fire. Therefore, Abraham has brought with him the three orders that are in the Church. He has brought with him two lads and his lad.

In every church you will have those who are the Abraham type – they are the total servants, total obedience, totally committed to do whatever God says. He is my daily bread. Abraham is a type of total obedience and faith and Isaac is the submissive one. The two servants were never called on to scale the mountain. These two lads were left at the foot of the mountain. They never had it in their hearts to scale the mountain. They were not following the voice of God. They were simply doing what they were asked to do and were not in a relationship with God to the degree that Abraham or Isaac was. In every Church there are people who do not clap their hands, do not worship, do not sing, do not teach, do not lead singing, etc. Some people have gone as far as they can go in their relationship with God. In addition, these factors are in their lives and it is not for you and me to decide who is going to stay at the foot of the mountain. You and I must purpose in our hearts that we will scale that mountain.

Many times, we are continually asking ourselves this question, what should I be doing for the Lord when the trumpet sounds?

I will tell you what we need to be doing – we need to be obeying God.

We need to be faithful to God and faithful to the things God has given us clarity on. The Apostle Paul advised us to exercise our senses so we can discern good from evil.

Hebrews 5:14 6:1 But strong meat belongeth to them that are of full age, even those who by reason of use have their senses exercised to discern both good and evil. Therefore leaving the principles of the doctrine of Christ let us go on unto perfection; not laying again the foundation of repentance from dead works and of faith toward God.

Sometimes we have need for someone else to teach us. Let us go on to perfection, let us step on out in obedience to God. I have prayed that you make it and that you make it with the struggle between Isaac and Ishmael. You know that the children of the bondwoman are many more than the children of the true wife.

Genesis 22:4,5 Then on the third day, Abraham lifted up his eyes and saw the place afar off. And Abraham said unto his young men, Abide ye here with the ass; and I and the lad will go yonder, and worship, and come again to you.

Abraham said there are two things that they are going to do. He said, "We are going to go worship and we will come back." Because Abraham knew that God had promised through Isaac, so if

God has to raise him up, He will raise him up. Whatever God has to do, He will do because I have a promise greater than this. We have a promise greater than death and that is wonderful. Those that were standing there at the foot of the mountain heard these words that Abraham said, "we shall be together again!" We will have life beyond this storm, beyond this test, beyond this trial here and we will come together again.

Genesis 22:6 And Abraham took the wood of the burnt offering and laid it upon Isaac his son; and he took the fire in his hand and a knife; and they went both of them together.

Abraham took the wood that the price was going to be paid on and he handed it over and said, "Isaac you will carry this." And the lovely Son of God carried His cross, the cross was put on the Son's shoulder, but the Father said, "I will take care of the knife and I will take care of the fire." Jesus said it is out of your hands and in the Father's hands. Your life and my life are in the Father's hands. He will never leave us alone. I know many times we get anxious and concerned and we get fearful about material things and things that can happen to us. Nevertheless, remember the father keeps the knife himself and he keeps the fire himself. He is going to carry the knife and the fire. Now Abraham is too old to do that. In reality he should have turned to those two lads and said, "One of you carry the knife and the other carry the fire for this old man. It is all I can do to get up the mountain. I am 125 years old."

When it comes to true love, you do not turn it over to someone else. Abraham said, "I will carry the knife. I will carry the fire and I will make the mountain." It makes me to know that nothing is going to happen in your life and mine, but what God will allow. God said, "I am with you always, even to the end of the world." The steps of the righteous are ordained of God and nothing shall overtake us. What can separate us from the love of God? (Romans 8:35.) The Father still has the knife in His hands, and thank God, He still has the fire that you and I need in the Church, that anointing of God. It is going to be a whole burnt offering, so we must crucify the flesh!

Isaac is coming to the altar, symbolically speaking, is you and I coming to the altar of God, presenting our bodies as a living sacrifice. The two-edged sword, the Word of God – knife – is thrust into the fleshly man. He dies and the spiritual man lives. At the altar of obedience and faith, the natural man will die before he will kneel there, and the spiritual man is deaf until he kneels there. When we know the truth and we step up to that altar of commitment to that truth, the natural man dies and the spiritual man becomes alive. So this is what is going to happen: the knife is going to penetrate the whole burnt offering, the flesh is going to die, and the fire is going to consume that body. That is what the Holy Ghost does to us – He consumes us, laminates us, and motivates us as we spearhead the program of God.

John the Baptist said that Jesus would baptize us with Holy Ghost and fire.

You will become a light in the night, a vehicle of God, a source; you will become the power that dispels the adversary. The Father holds the fire, and He holds the knife. Our sovereignty decides whether we take our cross, receive the knife, and burn with the fire of God.

The Son said, "Father not My will, but Thy will be done." He knew the Father's will on Calvary, so they drove the nails in His hands and feet and put the crown on His brow. They pierced His side and beat His back. Jesus bowed His head and said, "Father, it is finished. I have been the obedient Son, I have been the paschal lamb, and it is over."

When we come to the sunset of our lives, we can say that we have fought a good fight, kept the faith, finished our course, and have a crown of life. This is what is taking place here with Isaac.

Who is telling this story?

You know, the first five books were written by Moses. However, he was not there for this time with Abraham and Isaac. So he is therefore writing this for God. He is writing this on Sinai Mountain and God is telling this story. He is bragging on Abraham and Isaac; he is bragging on the whole bunch because of their obedience and their faith. When people are taking issue with this, they are taking issue with God.

2 Timothy 3:16 All scriptures are given by inspiration of God and are profitable for doctrine, for reproof, for correction, for instruction in righteousness:

Abraham obeyed God so that means that we can. Abraham had faith in God and that means that we can. The bottom line is that we are not excusable now that we have studied and understood this.

Genesis 22:7,8 And Isaac spake unto Abraham his father

and said, my father: and he said, here am I, my son. And he said behold the fire and the wood: but where is the lamb for a burnt Offering?

This is too much to comprehend!

I am sure that we all desire to be as obedient as was Isaac. There are many things that I do not understand and there were things that Isaac did not understand. Isaac said, "I can see the religious end to this thing. I see you have the fire, I see the knife, and I am carrying the wood, but where is the sacrifice? Well God had to put it in Abraham's heart, what to say concerning that matter. Someway and somehow, he already understood about the lamb sacrifice and remembered that he is the Father of the Hebrews. It began with him, and there was not a Hebrew before this time. Abraham is the Hebrew of the Hebrews.

Mountain of Moriah!

Scripture references:
Genesis 22:4,5 Then on the third day Abraham lifted up his eyes and saw the place afar off. And Abraham said unto his young men, Abide ye here with the ass; and I and the lad will go yonder and worship and come again to you.

Genesis 14:18,19,20	2 Chronicles 3:1
Genesis 22:2,9,10,11	Matthew 26:39
1 Samuel 15:14,22	Luke 21:36
1 Chronicles 21:1,2,15,24	Romans 12:1

The Lord had admonished Abraham, who was living at Beer-Sheba at the time, to go to the mountain that He would show him.

Genesis 22:2 And he said, take now thy son, thine only son Isaac, whom thou lovest and get thee into the land of Moriah; and offer him there for a burnt offering upon one of the mountains which I will tell thee of.

This is an area of mountains or a high hill, one of which is Calvary; on the other is Sinai, and this one area which Abraham and Isaac will venture to will be Moriah. Moriah was the region or the town of Salem at this time and was mentioned four times in the Bible. Each of these is a progressive work. Now if I fail to get this to you, then it will be difficult for you to understand some of the things that constitute the sons of the promise.

Therefore, Mount Moriah is going to become a geographical stepping-stone in an experience for us. Some of these other areas need explaining also; the feast days are spiritual experiences for us. Every piece of furniture that was in the Temple or Tabernacle depicted a spiritual experience for us and so is Mount Moriah. Nevertheless, you and I today have come here, because we want to know the way of escape.

Genesis 22:9,10,11 And they came to the place which God had told him of (Moriah); and Abraham built an altar there and laid the wood in order and bound Isaac his son and laid him on the altar upon the wood. And Abraham stretched forth his hand and took the knife to slay his son. And the angel of the Lord called unto him out of heaven and said Abraham, Abraham: and he said, Here am I.

In the next chapter, we are going to learn about Sarah's death. I want to point out the fact that she died in 1860 B.C. According to the opening verse in the 23rd chapter, she died at the age of 127 years.

Sarah was 90 years old when Isaac was born. That means Isaac was 37 years old when Sarah died. Sarah's death took place twelve years after the 22nd chapter of Genesis when Abraham was tested. So Isaac was 25 years old when he was offered by his father on Mount Moriah. He was bound, put on the altar, knowing his father had a knife in his hand to take his life. Still, he laid his life on the altar because his father admonished him to do so. When we compare the circumstances of Abraham and Issac with the story of Jesus Christ, there are some important differences. A Hebrew reaches manhood at thirty. That is the reason John the Baptist and Jesus could not literally enter their ministry until they were thirty years of age. Isaac being 25, when he was offered, places the attention on Abraham, rather than Isaac. Jesus being crucified at 33 ½ yrs. old places the attention on Christ instead of the Father.

Isaac laid down his life on the altar, because his father had admonished him to do it, (Isaac being submissive and 25 years of age) not that he would not have done it! However, Christ had to be offered of his free will. He had to go willingly to the cross at the age of 33 ½ years. In looking at these scriptures, you will notice, both are of the Father's will.

Mathew 26:39 And he went a little farther and fell on his face and prayed saying, O my father, if it be possible, let this cup pass from me: nevertheless, not as I will, but as thou wilt.

Mount Moriah, means what Jehovah, had made one to see! There are things that Jehovah has made for us to see, it is in a relationship with the Lord Jesus Christ and God has made a way of escape. However, not all are interested in turning aside from the flesh and finding the way of escape. They will wait and cry with the Egyptians at the passing of the death angel.

Luke 21:36 Watch ye therefore and pray always, that ye may be accounted worthy to escape all these things that shall come to pass and to stand before the Son of Man.

(Read all of Luke chapter 21)

There must be accountability on our part, and to become accountable we must understand what Jehovah wants us to see. We then become accountable and can do something about it.

There are four things that God makes available in the plan of Salvation. It is explained in the life of Abraham, because Abraham had sons of the promise.

We are the sons of promise and our children will be the sons of promise, but there are things we must understand. Those who are sincerely interested in these things will find the way of escape. Those that are not interested will take a course of lesser resistance and run down the road without a clue or care about their eternity. There are things in each of us that need to be expressed like who we are, what we see, what we believe, where we stand, what our desires are, and so on. As I was praying, the Lord impressed on me an expression saying...

The price that we pay for life's games we play.

The choices we make effect our eternity as well as our children in greater magnitude than I am able to explain.

I. Abraham Gave Tithe to Melchizedek:

The first time that Moriah is mentioned in the Bible is when Abraham returns from the slaughter of the kings. He comes to Mount Moriah and out of Salem where a man came to meet him. His name was Melchizedek. He brought bread, wine, and provisions for Abraham's men. Abraham, though not commissioned to do so, gave Melchizedek tithe on Mount Moriah.

Genesis 14:18,19,20 And Melchizedek king of Salem brought forth bread and wine: and he was the priest of the most high God. And he blessed him and said, Blessed be Abram of the most high God, possessor of heaven and earth: And blessed be the most high God, which hath delivered thine enemies into thy hand. And he gave him tithes of all.

God said, "Abraham out of your heart you want to give me a tithe." Melchizedek is king–priest. The only other king–priest in the Bible is Jesus Christ.

God watched Abraham pay a tenth to Melchizedek. With every test he moves higher on the scale in eternity. We must pray, listen, and act in order to progress and understand God's will.

Personal reference:

I want to tell you that before God could bless us the way that He has, He had to do a work in my heart. Now, I am not here preaching on tithes. I am telling you about hurdles. I found myself on bended knees praying, "God I want to give tithes, not pay tithes, but give them." It belongs to God. Giving tithes is just a test to see if we are honest or not.

Brother Reed, why would you teach people who do not have anything to give tithes?

While in Africa, I was asked why I teach about tithing to people who have nothing. There will always be poverty until we learn the principles of God. Pastor Moses in Africa wanted us to teach his pastors about tithes.

This was difficult for me to teach one hundred preachers who did not know where supper is coming from to give tithes.

I used a visual example to help explain the concept. I used ten beans and explained nine of these beans belong to you and one bean belongs to God.

God wants to use us in the kingdom, but we must be obedient and honest. There is no place for thieves in the kingdom. That is hard to say to one hundred people who are looking at you, and they do not have two washers to rub together, much less two coins. Nonetheless, the men learned when they were given help by missions to give one-tenth back to God.

I came to the place where I told God, "I am willing to do anything in order to be blessed." My wife and I scraped an old house. I fired up an old makeshift paint rig and we painted a house. We earned enough to begin giving to God. From then on, whatever money came in, we gave one-tenth to God.

I don't want to go through this again, I've had enough of that! After this hurdle, we were able to move on and up with God.

Abraham faced another hurdle.

II. Abraham offered Isaac on Mount Moriah:

Genesis 22:2 And he said," Take now thy son, thine only son Isaac whom thou lovest and get thee into the land of Moriah; and offer him there for a burnt offering upon one of the mountains which I will tell thee of.

It was a three-day journey. It was a time of salvation, sanctification, and the Holy Ghost. This type of obedience sets us apart from where we live to where we obey. This is total obedience. Isaac was a complete burnt offering, not a sin offering. The offering represents the totality of us – soul, spirit, and body.

Romans 12:1 I beseech you therefore brethren, by the mercies of God, that ye present your bodies a living sacrifice, holy, acceptable unto God which is your reasonable service.

The Lord asked Abraham to give Him his son, Isaac. We must love God more than things of this world - mother, sister, father, brother – and present them to God saying, "This is Yours." The two servants stayed at the foot of Mount Moriah.

Abraham now takes his son Isaac and puts the wood on his son, symbolizing the cross that Jesus carried.

Abraham (The Father) carried the knife, representing the choice of life and death. The fire symbolizes the anointing of God.

Mountain of Moriah!

Abraham, 125 years old, scaled Mount Moriah with the knife and fire. He carried the knife and fire. What went on in heaven while Abraham and Isaac scaled the mountain? What a heavy load Abraham must have carried in his heart; obedience can be an extremely heavy load to bear.

1 Samuel 15:14,22 And Samuel said, what meaneth then this bleating of the sheep in mine ears and the lowing of the oxen which I hear? And Samuel said, Hath the Lord as great delight in burnt offerings and sacrifices as in obeying the voice of the Lord? Behold to obey is better than sacrifice and to harken than the fat of rams.

Obedience is still better than sacrifice.

Whenever Samuel came to Saul and asked, "Have you obeyed God?" Saul replied, "Yes, I have." Samuel then asked, "What is the bleating of the sheep and the lowing of the oxen that I hear?"

III. Jebusite:

This is the third thing that is mentioned about Mount Moriah. This was the original threshing floor of the Jebusites.

Do you remember the great sin of David?

He numbered Israel.

1 Chronicles 21:1,2 And Satan stood up against Israel and provoked David to number Israel. And David said to Joab and to the rulers of the people, Go, number Israel from Besheba even to Dan; and bring the number of them to me, that I may know it.

The story goes on, and in verse seven we learn that

God is not pleased with David and gave him a choice of punishments. David took his punishment from the Lord.

1 Chronicles 21:15 (in-part) 24 And an Angel of the Lord stood by the threshing floor of Ornan the Jebusite. And King David said to Ornan, Nay; but I will verily but it for the full price: for I will not take that which is thine for the Lord, nor offer burnt offerings without cost.

David pays full price for the threshing floor of Ornan and builds an altar to God.

2 Chronicles 3:1 Then Solomon began to build the house of the Lord at Jerusalem in Mount Moriah, where the Lord appeared unto David his father, in the place that David had prepared in the threshing floor of Ornan the Jebusite.

IV. *Solomon:*

Solomon built the Lord's Temple on Mount Moriah, Salem, City of David, Jerusalem. Solomon is the son of the promise, and he is the first man that the Bible says loved God.

Thou Hast Obeyed My Voice

Scripture references:
Genesis 22:17,18 That in blessing, I will bless thee, and in multiplying, I will multiply thy seed as the stars of the heaven and as the sand which is upon the seashore; and thy seed shall possess the gate of his enemies. And in thy seed shall all the nations of the earth be blessed; because thou hast obeyed my voice.

Genesis 22:13,14,15,16   Acts 7:58
Matthew 16:18,19   John 1:2,3

As we study there is always additional revelation. That is why I encourage you to be open-minded and always leave the door open for additional revelation. There is the Word of God, and then there is the Word of God in depth. There are the deeper things, as it is with Abraham, who was tested and tried, in building an altar and offering Isaac. Each of us needs to build an altar. The altar is where God and man come together. That is depicted in the tabernacle and the temple. Within the Holiest of Holies, was the mercy seat, but one first had to pass the great brazen altar where the sacrifice is made. Then he had to pass the altar of incense where intimate time with Christ or God was shared. Until the cross and the death of Christ, the high priest went in to the mercy seat. This all has great implications and ramifications in our lives. We must still pass the brazen altar and make a sacrifice before we stand at the mercy seat. Some have not made the sacrifice. Their lives are still not sacrificed; commitment is just not there, especially in this hour of apostasy.

Genesis 22:13,14 And Abraham lifted up his eyes and

Who Are the Sons of the Promise?

looked and behold behind him a ram caught in a thicket by his horns: and Abraham went and took the ram and offered him up for a burnt offering in the stead of his son. And Abraham called the name of that place Jehovah-jireh: as it is said to this day, in the mount of the Lord it shall be seen.

Did you ever wonder what great deeds Abraham did? He really never had any great moments. The offering of Isaac was an act of obedience to God. Abraham was not a great leader or a man who scaled the ladder. He was simply a man who believed what God said, had faith, and was obedient. Abraham is an example to every one of us about what God desires, not to be great meteorites that illuminate the heavens, speed our way across a darkened world in the sense of here today and burnt out tomorrow. He is not calling on us to be someone great. This is not what He is teaching us in the life of Abraham. He is teaching us to just be obedient and faithful. Abraham's life was not an Elijah or Elisha, not a Jeremiah, Daniel, John the Baptist, nor a Simon Peter. He was just one who was obedient and faithful.

Genesis 22:15,16 And the angel of the Lord called unto Abraham out of heaven the second time, and said, by myself have I sworn saith the Lord, for because thou hast done this thing and hast not withheld thy son, thine only son:

God called Abraham on Mount Moriah; this is the second voice from God since Abraham was called to Mount Moriah. He had a knife drawn on Isaac. If God had not intervened, Isaac would have been a dead lad in just a few seconds. God spoke to Abraham and said to not touch him, and hold the knife right there. Abraham obeyed. After offering the ram, the angel said unto him the second time, "By myself have I sworn." In these next four verses hinges wisdom. He could not swear of anyone greater than Himself.

"Everything that is was made by Me and without Me nothing was made."

John 1:2,3 The same was in the beginning with God. All things were made by him; and without him was not any thing made that was made. In him was life; and the life was the light of men.

When heaven and earth are passed away, the earth will be renovated. In John's Revelation he tells us this and that the order of the heavens will change at the close of the Battle of Armageddon and be finalized at the close of the millennium. After all this has taken place, the earth will still be. Isn't that wonderful?

This covenant is not about how many camel, servants, or land you possess. This covenant is about us and our seed and this is what we are interested in. Your ministry, your spiritual and natural seed are waiting on our commitment and our relationship with God. They are waiting on us to step up to the altar and find ourselves standing in Abraham's shoes. God is no respecter of persons and He will do for us what He has done for anyone that has ever been. All we need to do is get close to our altar and make our sacrifice. We are then sons of the promise. Abraham is standing by his altar and his son is submissive to the call of God on his life. Isaac was lying there bound waiting for the knife. Abraham is wise enough to understand that it is you and your lineage that is more important than everything else in the world. I am here to talk about you and your lineage.

He did not talk about the seed or the sons of the seed of Ishmael. Ishmael was not the one on the altar; Isaac was the one on the altar. It will come through the man who is on the altar; it must come from the man who was hanging on the tree.

There is no other name given. You either come through

the Man that was hanging on the tree or you will not get there.

This is now between Abraham, his son, and his son's son, and the lineage as they learn obedience. Isaac was a type of Christ; he was a very meek, mild mannered man. He was obedient and God fearing. He would dig a well, the enemy would come, and he would move and dig another one. However, he has a son, Jacob, who was not as passive. Before the blessing could flow through Jacob, he had to experience storms and the night of wrestling with the angel.

Would Jacob have been as conniving if Rebecca had not coached him?

This is a very difficult and an unanswerable question. Nevertheless, notice one thing- he was wrestling before he got here. Jacob and Esau were wrestling before they were born and they have never stopped wrestling since. We do not see this behavior in Rebecca or in Isaac, so we will have to wait and see where it came from. That is about all I can do to judge some of my behaviors and genetic makeup. That is the reason why the Jews will go through the night of tribulations, wrestling with the man of war. They are not submissive and it has to stop until they become submissive. That is true in the lives of our sons and daughters. Until we become submissive, we will have to learn obedience, and there is no substitute for obedience. None! We substitute mercy, grace, and the love of God for obedience and it will not work. We are either obedient or disobedient. Whatever God must do to make me obedient, He will do it. It was God touching the life of each generation as they came, but it had to start with Abraham at the altar. In addition, God dealt with the most vital part of any man's life, his descendents.

Genesis 22:17 That in blessing, I will bless thee and in multiplying, I will multiply thy seed as the stars of the heaven and as the sand which is upon the seashore; and thy seed shall possess the gate of his enemies;

Now this is a great word of prophecy:

"Thy seed shall possess the gate of his enemies." This means that whoever controls the gate of the city controls the city. Do you remember when the angels came to Sodom and Gomorrah? They spoke with those that were sitting at the gate including Lot. He was brought in because he was a good man to judge the people, and they needed it, but Lot did not do it!

Do you remember Saul of Tarsus was making havoc with the church?

Acts 7:58 And cast him out of the city and stoned him: and the witnesses laid down their clothes at a young mans feet, whose name was Saul.

Saul of Tarsus was at the gate and they brought in Stephen. When they accused Stephen, they threw their coats at Paul's feet. It was as if he was holding their coats – he must approve as an elder at the gate. They accused Stephen saying, "This man is against the Mosaic law, the prophets, and the Sanhedrin." Saul said, "Give me your coat." That gesture suggested stoning Stephen. That was his approval of Stephen being stoned. He was at the gate.

The Lord is saying to Abraham, "May thy seed possess the gate." Throughout the life of Israel, when they worshiped idols, sinned, and backslid separating from God, they lost control of the gate. This is the how the Assyrians took Israel captive; they lost control of the gate. One hundred years later, the world empire – the Babylonians – took control of the gate when Nebuchadnezzar broke the walls of Jerusalem. Throughout the Bible, in Jerusalem, when it says, "Near the gate of the Virgins, by the Sheep gate, the Samaritan gate, the eastern gate." That refers to who holds control.

Who Are the Sons of the Promise?

In our lives today we have five gates – the eye gate and the other four senses. Ninety percent of all we know comes through the eye gate, and in all we observe we must choose to be obedient or disobedient. My prayer for you today is for you to possess the gate, to set no evil thing before your eyes, and to not approve the things of this world. God is telling us not only to posses our gates, but to go out and invade their kingdom. This is not talking about making war. Remember Jesus was talking to the disciples and He said, "I will give you the keys to the kingdom, and the gates of hell cannot prevail against it."

Hell's gates stand there and on the other side of that our loved ones, not the ones that are already in hell. Like Isaac, if God had not stopped Abraham, Isaac was as good as dead. Any person that is lost, unless something happens, is in hell.

I am giving you the keys. The Church is a battering ram and the gates of hell cannot stand against it. This is not saying any acts of mercy extend beyond the grave, but simply that we have loved ones outside the ark of safety, behind the gates of hell, who live in sin and the Church is God's antidote. He said the gates of hell cannot stand against the battering ram of the Church. God has promised me, because we have obeyed, that I will see my loved ones brought to the Lord. We are the sons of the promise, and may your seed and my seed possess the gate. The Lord tells us the seeds of the promise or the sons of the promise can also possess the enemy's gate. I've heard the average person influences seventy-five to one hundred twenty-five people. The least influential person in the world, likened it unto a man who is on skid row, influences six people.

My challenge to you is now that we know that we are sons of the promise, to stand up and begin to reach out our tent stakes, and believe God to bring our seventy-five to one hundred and twenty-five. With our faith, understanding of the Word of God, knowledge that we are the sons of the promise, altar of commitment, willing to present ourselves as living sacrifice holy and acceptable to God, we will win our hundred and twenty-five. We are the Church, we are the answer for this dying world, and we are in the paths of people to witness about Jesus Christ.

How important are you in the life of that individual that is lost? Unless you become that battering ram that reaches them, they are lost without you! They will be lost eternally without you. You are the laborer in someone's path, are you not?

Genesis 22:18 And in thy seed shall all the nations of the earth be blessed; because thou hast obeyed my voice.

Everyone will be blessed because Abraham obeyed God. There is a blessing in our obedience to those who come across our path. Without obedience, the blessing will never arrive.

Therefore, I leave you with this from the beatitudes (or the attitude that should be). "Blessed are the pure in heart; blessed is he that hunger and thirst." There is a particular blessing that God has intended for you to receive in this world and the world to come.

Lineage & Bloodline of Abraham

Scripture references:
Genesis 23:9,11,13 That he may give me the cave of Machpelah, which he hath, which is in the end of his field, for as much money as it is worth he shall give it me for a possession of a burying place amongst you.
Nay my lord hear me: the field I give thee and the cave that is therein I give thee; (in-part)
But if thou will give it, I pray thee, hear me: I will give thee money for the field. (in-part)

Genesis 22:20,23   Matthew 7:13,14
Genesis 23:1,2,3,4,5,6   Matthew 18:21
Revelations 3:21 & 7:9

We have dealt with the offering of Isaac on the altar, and we thank the Lord for letting us understand the revelation in this chapter. We see the necessity of being submissive and obedient, as Isaac was submissive and obedient. Because Abraham and Isaac were obedient, the promise of their lineage is held true. Now we can move on to the next generation.

Obeying the voice of God has become too small of an issue among us Christians. When we find ourselves making choices for ourselves, we find ourselves getting away from God. We must be committed and follow the Word. When you begin to deviate a little, then a little more, soon much demands more and we are drifting down the current of life. Then nothing is quite right, and our attitudes turn that there is nothing quite wrong. We want to everyday bring ourselves into that line of obedience to God. We need to ask God, "What would you have me do today?" If we our nation, our lineage, and our children are to be blessed of

God, then we are going to have to obey the voice of God. It is that simple. I know that everything brings forth after its own kind, so if we are God's kind, then we will bring forth after our kind, faithful and obedient.

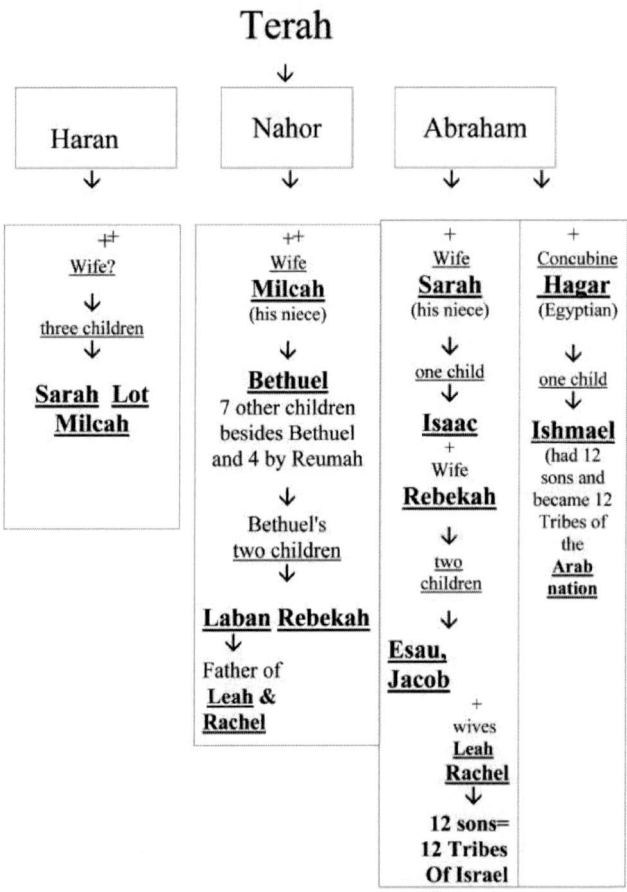

This all started with Terah. He had three sons, Haran the oldest, then Nahor, and then Abraham. We understand that Haran's wife is not mentioned. Haran had three children, Sarah, Lot, and Milcah. Each is very important in the lineage and bloodline.

We see Nahor marries Milcah his niece. Abraham

Who Are the Sons of the Promise?

marries his niece Sarah, who is the daughter of Haran.

Then there is Lot, who should have been left in Haran, but Abraham took him with him into Canaan's Land.

Nahor had eight children, but one, Bethuel, bore Laban and Rebekah.

We will talk about Rebekah in the 24th chapter of Genesis. Rebekah marries Isaac and to that union was born Esau and Jacob. Out of Jacob, who marries Leah and Rachel, come the Twelve Tribes of Israel.

Under Hagar is Ishmael, who had twelve sons, which became the twelve tribes of the Arabian nation. When Abram was interceding for Ishmael, asking God, "What about my son Ishmael?" God said," He too shall be a nation and have twelve sons." We did not list them here and the Moslems will feel left out, but they are not the bloodline.

It seems in those days, because of the population and God's intent, that this intermarriage of families did not have the effect that it does today. Most marriages were arranged; Abraham arranged the marriage of Isaac.

However, we do not see it in Jacobs's life. Jacobs finds a woman he is in love with, works seven years for her, and gets her sister. Most marriages were arranged, some were not, so it is not a law, but a strong tie. If one marries out of the bloodline, that person was an outcast. We see that happening in Israel when the Assyrians took the Ten Tribes of Israel into captivity and left certain people to oversee that taxes were gathered and tribute was paid. They began to intermarry with the Assyrians. This is why the Jews look down on the Samaritans. A Samaritan was one of those in Israel who married into the Assyrian people. They called them dogs and half-breeds and all those ugly things. When Jesus came to the Well of Jacob and Jesus asked her for a drink of water, the woman was shocked and asked," Why would you a Jew even speak to me, a Samaritan?"

It was a sin for a Jew to speak to a Samaritan. This law is why they lost their relationship and the promise of God. God told them to be a priestly people. They were guarding their bloodline, thinking, "If we make these ridged rules none of us will speak to a heathen, a gentile, and will not intermarry."

That is why, even today, Bible scholars are looking for a Jew to be the

Antichrist, because they are so rigid regarding their bloodline. When the Babylonians came later and took Jerusalem into captivity for seven years, they were very rigid about never letting one of their children marry a Babylonian. Then Nehemiah and Ezra came back to build the walls of Jerusalem and the temple. They came back a pure bloodline people.

This is similar to the Church world today. The clouds of compromise and worldliness are threatening the Church. We must keep the standard of holiness, but love others where they are, yet not become as they are.

Genesis 22:20,23 And it came to pass after these things, that it was told Abraham saying, Behold, Milcah, she hath also born children unto thy brother Nahor; And Bethuel begat Rebekah; these eight Milcah did bear to Nahor, Abraham brother.

Notice that Nahor and Milcah bore a son Bethuel and he bore a daughter whose name is Rebekah.

We understand now that Rebekah is going to play a major role in the sons of the promise.

Genesis 23:1 And Sarah was a hundred and seven and twenty years old: these were the years of the life of Sarah.

Who Are the Sons of the Promise?

Sarah is 127 years old and Abraham is 137 years old; he is ten years older than Sarah. God gave Abraham a promise and that promise is working. Sarah passes away, and after her death and mourning, he marries another woman and has six more sons.

How many sons did Abraham have?

Most people would say two, but in reality, he had eight!

Were these six excluded?

No, they were not of the bloodline, but they have a place and role. These six sons are depicted in the tribulation time of the great multitude that no man can number. They fall in this role, they are not excluded, but they are not following as sons of the promise. Sarah is 127 years old and is depicted as the Church. The Church now steps out of the action. This is a subject all its own. The church is stepping off of the stage of action; the bloodline is going to follow. Next chapter, we will see the product of the Church and the role that the product plays, because the 24th chapter of Genesis is totally given to the Bride Hood order. The Church as it has been known will cease to be.

Who owns the promise land?

Abraham and his seed. We are spiritually in the promise land, as we are under grace and mercy; the promises are given to us freely. Every promise in the book is mine. Salvation is ours, sanctification is ours, the Holy Ghost is ours, the gifts of the spirit are ours, and the power of agreement is ours. We are in the promise land; we are in the best days this world has ever seen. The Church played its role and there must be a place for the Church. Of course, we are symbolically speaking. What did Abraham do with the body of Sarah?

Genesis 23:2, 3,4,5,6 And Sarah died in Kirjatharba; the same as Hebron in the land of Canaan: and Abraham came to mourn for Sarah and to weep for her. And Abraham stood up from before his dead and spake unto the sons of Heth saying, I am a stranger and s sojourner with you: give me a possession of a burying place with you, that I may bury my dead out of my sight. And the children of Heth answered Abraham, saying unto him, Hear us, my Lord: thou art a mighty prince among us: in the choice of our sepulchers bury thy dead; none of us shall withhold from thee his sepulcher, but that thou mayest bury thy dead.

Abraham is in the promise land and it is time to bury his wife. You would think he would say, "This is my land and I can bury my wife wherever I want to," but there is a lesson here for us today.

We have this mental concept... all I have to do is get saved, go to heaven and walk on the streets of gold, and I am going to be on those streets of Gold forever and ever. That is all you have to do is name the name of the Lord. The only problem is that is contrary to the scriptures. How many people will tell you, "All I want to do is stay out of hell and that is it"? What a sad commentary.

Every one of us is going to be rewarded according to our labors. Now if there were any man under God's heaven who shouldn't have to buy a place for the Church (Sarah) to be buried, it should have been Abraham.

However, getting saved does not put you into the position to receive rewards; you are going to have to purchase your reward, right here in the promise land.

If we want to receive rewards, judge over a city or ten cities or a nation, if we are going to be a priest or king for God in the world to come, then we are going to pay the price, right here in the promise land. Eternal life is free; there will be people who are servants of God throughout eternity. They have eternal life, the thief on the cross; salvation was free, but on what status will he spend eternity? He received eternal life only, no rewards, and will be a servant throughout eternity.

There are the different levels of Heaven, in the seven letters to the seven Churches of Asia from salvation, to the Church of Ephesus, and unto the Laodicean Church. This was written in Revelation.

Revelations 3:21 To him that overcometh will I grant to sit with me in my throne, even as I also overcame and am set down with my Father in his throne.

On what level will you be?

We are going to have to pay the price here in the promise land. Jesus said to the rich young ruler when he asked, "What shall I do to inherit eternal life?" Jesus replied:

Matthew 18:21 Jesus said unto him, if thou wilt be perfect, go and sell that thou hast and give to the poor and thou shalt have treasure in heaven: and come follow me.
"Take what you have, give it to the poor, take up your cross, follow Me, and great will be your reward in Heaven." Heaven is not a pie in the sky.

The Bible says that without holiness, no man shall see God. However, every eye will see Jesus, every knee will bow to Jesus, every tongue shall confess to Jesus, but without holiness you will never get to go to the Throne Room of God. It is said that the Bible contradicts itself; it does not, and without holiness no man will see God.

However, every eye will see Jesus, the sinner will see Jesus, the drunkard will see Jesus, the gambler will see

Jesus, and the whoremonger will see Jesus, and they will be judged. That is why Jesus says...

Matthew 7:13,14 Enter ye in at the strait gate: for wide is the gate and broad is the way that leadeth to destruction and many there be which go in thereat. Because strait is the gate and narrow is the way, which leadeth unto life and few there be that find it.

Then in Revelation the Bible says...

Revelation 7:9 After this I beheld and lo, a great multitude, which no man could number, of all nations and kindred and people and tongues, stood before the lamb, clothed with white robes and palms in their hands;

It appears the Bible contradicts itself; but it does not. These are servants on the new earth! There is a gate to that city, but few will enter. You and I, friend, are going to pay a price if we want to possess inside of that promise land, The New Jerusalem. This is why we have been given this allotment of time. Remember the Prodigal Son committed two sins, one against his father and one against Heaven. We do not know how many days God has given us on this earth to work for Him. If you and I will spend our days working for Him, we are not sinning against Heaven; we are laying up treasures in heaven. But if we go out and live the way the world is living and do the things that the world is doing, we are sinning against Heaven. We are sinning against that opportunity to lay up treasures in Heaven.

Abraham had to purchase a place in the promise land so that he would have his Church, his bride right there. Incidentally, Abraham was buried there, Isaac was buried there, and Jacob was buried there. In this twenty-third chapter, Abraham is taking time to tell us that if we want an eternal reward for our labors, there is a work for us to do now. The sons of the promise are going to be the sons of the Church; if we are not sons of the Church, we will not be sons of the promise. I am not saying that you are lost; if we are not faithful to the God and the Church, we are not going to be sons of the promise.

Abraham & Eliezer

Scripture references:
Genesis 24:3,4
And I will make thee swear by the Lord the God of heaven and the God of the earth that thou shalt not take a wife unto my son of the daughters of the Canaanites, among whom I dwell: But thou shalt go unto my country and to my kindred and take a wife unto my son Isaac. And if the woman will not be willing to follow thee, then thou shalt be clear from this my oath only bring not my son thither again.

Genesis 24:1, 2,5,6,7,8,10,13,14,15,18,19
Matthew 5:17
John 4:23,24

In the Old Testament there are several people who project or portray Jesus Christ. They give us a foreshadow of Christ. These are Joseph, Isaac, Moses, Melchizedek and the third Angel. Isaac is numbered high on that list. What are some of the things that makes us know that he was a foreshadow, a symbol, or type of Christ? He was a servant, he was a sacrifice, and he was placed on the altar, as Christ was hung on the cross. He was that meek man and in our lesson today he is going to be portraying Christ in the sense that he gets a bride.

This 24th chapter of the Book of Genesis is just one of those that stands out there by itself, because there are very few statements or things that transpire in this 24th chapter that does not directly relate to the scenario of the rapture and the bride. Because of the day and the hour and because of the eternal picture, we need to really understand everything in the 24th chapter of the Book of Genesis.

Who Are the Sons of the Promise?

Genesis 24:1,2,3,4 And Abraham was old and well stricken in age: and the Lord had blessed Abraham in all things. And Abraham said unto his eldest servant of his house, that ruled over all that he had, Put I pray thee, thy hand under my thigh: And I will make thee swear by the Lord, the God of heaven, and the God of earth, that thou shalt not take a wife unto my son of the daughters of the Canaanites, among whom I dwell: But thou shalt go unto my country and to my kindred and take a wife unto my son Isaac.

There are many things being said. We learn it is the end of an era, an age, or a setting. This is a time of change for Abraham. This is not the end of Abraham's life; in fact, he remarries and has more children.

We come to the end of a sequence of events that will climax with events yet to transpire. He requests the person who is over all his treasures to place his hand under his thigh and swear.

In those days, they thought that the intent of our conduct came from the lower part of our belly. Later they brought it up to the heart. During Abraham's day, they felt like those things were manifested from the abundance of the inner part of man. They tell me our greeting "How are you?" originated from the greeting "How is your colon?" Sounds strange, does it not? It was once thought the source of life came from the colon.

Abraham has called in his eldest servant.

Who is this eldest servant?

Eliezer. His name means one along side, a helper.

Where did he come from?

Damascus, city of Praise!

Who were Eliezer's mom and dad?

They were the servants of Abraham. After Abraham had left Haran and was coming to Canaan land, they stopped off and camped one night just outside Damascus. This couple had a son and named him Eliezer. This has a great prophetic overtone.

What is Damascus? City of praise!

What is Canaan? Promise land!

Leaving the city of sin and coming to the promise land is a picture of salvation. We are in the promise land, and we have come to the place where we praise God with a perfect praise, and then and only then, do we get the Holy Ghost.

It is necessary for us to understand then that Eliezer, born unto Abraham's servants, grew up and became such a man that Abraham entrusted all that he had into his hands.

Now you remember back in our study when God and Abraham were talking together about Abraham having a son and Abraham said to God, "How is it that I have no son? All I have is this Eliezer." Abraham was saying to God, "This Eliezer is all I have."

It is like today a person who speaks in tongues and they do not reach any new births, or reach any souls. They just get the Holy Ghost and blend in instead of letting the Holy Ghost bring them out into the real purpose of life which is to build disciples, It is a reproducing cell. So, Abraham is saying, "God I have this servant, but is that all there is to this? Should I not have a son?" This is what we are saying. I do not mean that to be a burden to you, because the Holy Ghost in you will do a work in other people's lives.

Abraham now has this servant who has grown up and

showed himself wisely. He conducted himself wisely and he was given all that Abraham had; it was in his charge.

Now we are living in this Holy Ghost dispensation, and all of the gifts of the Spirit and all of the application of God come to us through the Spirit. That is the reason Jesus said to the woman at the well in Samaria, "The time was and now is that the true worshipers will worship Me in spirit and in truth."

John 4:23,24 But the hour cometh and now is, when the true worshipers shall worship the Father in Spirit and in truth: for the father seeketh such to worship him. God is a Spirit and they that worship him must worship him in spirit and in truth.

The Holy Ghost is the one who convicts us. He applies the blood of Christ to our sins. The Holy Ghost is the one that sanctifies us, applying the blood to our adamnic nature, and the Holy Ghost is the one who comes in and takes His abode within us.

Therefore, this is the Holy Ghost dispensation. We are seeing this now in the time that we are living, but God gave us a preview of it in the day of Abraham.

So Abraham is now down at Beer-sheba, and he has called in Eliezer. We are at the well of water or salvation, and God has beckoned in the Holy Ghost. He is saying to the Holy Ghost, "Now you swear to Me that you will go back yonder and You will bring a bride up here to My Son. Now you are not to get a bride here from where He is. You are to go back and bring Him a bride from My people, the true sons of Abraham."

In addition, we are the true sons of Abraham; we are the true followers of the Hebrews.

So he is back here now, right today as I speak, gathering a bride for Jesus Christ, his Isaac.

Genesis 24:5 And the servant said unto him, Peradventure the woman will not be willing to follow me unto this land: must I need bring thy son again unto the land from whence thou camest?

Eliezer says to Abraham, "What if the woman is not willing to be bride hood material? Peradventure her heart is not in being a bride and in pleasing you and Isaac?"

Therefore, I want you to know that the Bride is going to be a people whose hearts are given to the cause.

Genesis 24:6, 7, 8 And Abraham said unto him, Beware thou that bring not my son thither again. The Lord God of Heaven, which took me from my father's house and from the land of my kindred and which spake unto me, and that sware unto me saying, unto thy seed will I give this land; he shall send his angel before thee and thou shalt take a wife unto my son from thence. And if the woman will not be willing to follow thee, then thou shalt be clear from this my oath: only bring not my son thither again.

Abraham said to Eliezer, "If her heart is not in it, forget the whole thing."

What a statement. Do not force her, pressure her, or lay a guilt trip on her to become bride hood material. It has to be a choice of the heart, or she will come under another order. Eliezer swore to him concerning this matter.

Genesis 24:10 And the servant took ten camels of the camels of his master and departed; for all the goods of his master were in his hand: and he arose and went to Mesopotamia, unto the city of Nahor.

Eliezer gathers up ten camels, which were the vehicles

of the wilderness. These are the Ten Commandments. Not only did Eliezer ride these ten camels, but also Rebekah came back on those ten camels.

I thought the Bible said that Jesus came to fulfill the law?

Right, but notice what He said prior to that. He did not come to destroy the law; He came to fulfill the law.

Matthew 5:17 Think not that I am come to destroy the law or the prophets: I am not come to destroy, but to fulfill.

"The law will be satisfied in Me," said Jesus, "and if you are in Me then it will be satisfied in you." In the Sermon on the Mount, the Beatitudes (Matthew 5:1-12), Jesus was talking to His disciples. He took those Ten Commandments in essence, and throughout His lifetime, He magnified them. Some people would say, "I do not want to be strapped to the Ten Commandments." We are living above the Ten Commandments; we are living higher than the Commandments. We do not even worry about the Ten Commandments; our commitment to Christ took us above them.

Jesus magnified them and Jesus' death made them honorable. In other words, the Commandment that says, "Thou shall not commit adultery," Jesus magnified that by saying, "If you look on a woman and lust after her, you have already committed adultery."

I never touched her and she never touched me, so how can I be guilty?

Well that is a two way street – it is in the heart. That is the reason pornography is a multibillion dollar industry is because who knows the heart. It is desperately wicked above all things. Jesus magnified the law. In the old economy, we lived holy on Sunday or on Saturday, but under this, we live holy every day of the week.

Under the law, He lists these many things that we cannot do, but if you look at it, Christians today are living above that, and I thank God that we are.

Nevertheless, Eliezer gathered up these ten camels, (that is the reason he told us how many there were), because those old commandments were the means that they traveled across the wilderness. By that I mean the children of Israel could not have made the journey, in even pleasing God, without the commandments. Those commandments brought them across the wilderness. Now we are under the Holy Ghost, and the Holy Ghost brings us above that. The commandments are under us, and we thank God for that. Eliezer gathers the ten camels and heads back to find the woman.

When Eliezer comes back, he stops at the well. He does not go out to the bleak desert floor; he goes to where the living water is, and that is where the Bride is going to be. She is going to be nurtured in the House of God, and she is going to be bringing all that she is in charge of to the House of God where the living water is.

That is why the scripture says forsake not the assembling of yourselves together. Be sure and do that as we see the day approaching.

Genesis 24:13,14 Behold, I stand here by the well of water; and the daughters of the men of the city come out to draw water: And let it come to pass, that the damsel to whom I shall say, Let down thy picture, I pray thee, that I may drink; and she shall say, Drink and I will give thy camels drink also: let the same be she that thou hast appointed for thy servant Isaac; and thereby shall I know that thou hast showed kindness unto my master.

Eliezer comes to the well of water and he stands there and his camels are behind him. Those camels can drink from 40 to 50 gallons of water apiece. There are ten of them; if they just drink 30 gallons apiece, you can figure how many gallons that will be.

Eliezer said, "God I am here now at the well of water. I am here at that living source, that life giving source." That has to be for us to go on another day. It was the girls' job to keep the sheep. He said that in a little bit the virgins are going to be coming...

Remember when I told you that David was doing a girl's job. When Samuel came to Bethlehem, Jesse said, "Yes, here are my seven sons." Samuel then asked if there was not another one.

Jesse answered and said, "Yes, but he is doing a girl's job." Samuel replied, "Well I am not going to sit down until you get him in here."

Therefore, Rebekah comes in with the virgins of that hour who were keeping the sheep.

Eliezer had said unto the Lord – this is a conversation between the Holy Ghost and God – "Lord, I am going to ask these young ladies as they come by for a drink water, 'Give me a little of that, give me of that living substance.'

And that woman that You have picked out for me is going to be a willing-hearted servant. She is going to say to me, 'I will not only give you a drink of water sir, but I will water those ten camels.'"

As Eliezer was standing there, Rebekah walks by, and the Holy Ghost asks, "Could I have some living water?"

Genesis 24:15, 18, 19 And it came to pass before he had done speaking that behold Rebekah came out who was born to Bethuel, son of Milcah the wife of Nahor, Abraham's brother, with her pitcher upon her shoulder. And she said drink my Lord: and she hasted and let down her pitcher upon her hand and gave him drink.

And when she had done giving him drink, she said, I will draw water for thy camels also, until they have done drinking.

That is what is being asked of us today: "Can you do what needs to be done to give me a drink of that living water?"

Rebekah with a servant's heart said, "Sir, drink all that you want, and I will also water those Ten Commandments. I will put the Spirit of God to those Ten Commandments; I will put the Spirit of Life to those Ten Commandments."

I am sure Eliezer was in somewhat of a state of amazement.

Bear in mind that this well had about a fifteen-foot recess because it had been used so much and was worn down.

To get to the mouth of this well, you had to go down an embankment about fifteen feet. Then you had to drop that bucket down at least a hundred feet and draw up a gallon or two of water. That is not an easy chore, especially after tending sheep all day. Rebekah was tired. However, her heart was to serve, and she had a servant's heart. This is nothing less than a providential act; Eliezer never one time helped her with one bucket.

If she is going to be disgruntled, I am going to give her every opportunity to be disgruntled. If she is going to be negative, I am going to give her every opportunity to be negative.

Therefore, Rebekah drew this water, went out, and poured it in the trough; ten thirsty camels went to drinking. They could drink it quicker than she could draw it. I do not know how long she was there. Knowing that those camels would drink more than 30 gallons after coming across that desert, that is 300 gallons of water. Take 300 gallons of water and divide it by 2, and that is a lot of trips! That is a lot of water and a lot of work. It was already evening and she was already tired, but her heart took her beyond being tired.

Sarah's Tent

Scripture references:
Genesis 24:67   25:10
And Isaac brought her into his mother Sarah's tent and took Rebekah and she became his wife;
and he loved her: and Isaac was comforted after his mother's death.
The field which Abraham purchased of the sons of Heth: there was Abraham buried, and Sarah his wife.

Genesis 24:19,20,21,22	Ecclesiastes 9:10
Genesis 24:23,24,25,62	Revelation 1:13
Genesis 24:63,64,65,66	Revelation 14:14,15
Genesis 25:7,9,11	Revelation 19:12

I have thoroughly appreciated our journey through the life of Abraham. We are now in the closing of the 24th chapter of the Book of Genesis. In the 23rd chapter, Sarah was buried and Abraham will be buried with her in the 25th chapter. In Haran, Rebekah gives Eliezer a drink and waters the camels. This is saying that we can assist the Holy Ghost in much.

The Holy Ghost is here for everyone, but not everyone has Him. He is here to work in everyone's life, but He is not focused on everyone's life. This is why the Bible says when any two of us agree as touching any one thing, our Father in heaven will grant it. When you and your spouse or the pastor, siblings, or saint agrees concerning a matter in faith believing, then that focuses the eye of God. The vehicle of God in our day and time is the Holy Ghost. That brings the Holy Ghost to that individual conviction. Therefore, that is the reason that Rebekah gave Eliezer a drink of water. In addition, we give ourselves and what

Who Are the Sons of the Promise?

we have unto the Holy Ghost, and then He utilizes that to meet the need that is. We thank God for the Holy Ghost!

Genesis 24:19,20 And when she had done giving him drink, she said, I will draw water for thy camels also, until they have done drinking. And she hasted and emptied her pitcher into the trough, and ran again unto the well to draw water and drew for all his camels.

When that last old camel raised his head and there was still water in the trough, you know Eliezer became excited and beside himself. He reached over in the bag and began to draw out gold and silver. Rebekah did not have a clue about all that she was about to receive. She was doing it because it needed to be done and she had a servant's heart.

Now, if that were me, I would have stopped at the second bucket and said, "Eliezer, you and I take turns here buddy. Get a hold of that rope!" You have to understand that this was an intentional thing of God (providential act), because this is not a normal thing to do. There is no normality in this anywhere. Rebekah just kept on. I think that in my own life I realize that it is the attitude that will determine our altitude. There are many days that you and I have the opportunity to get the wrong attitude in Church and out of Church. Our attitude is very important because there is Someone higher than us, watching this. God was watching to see if Rebekah's attitude qualified her to be Isaac's wife, and she passed it! If our attitude is not right, we are going to be wasting our time. We have to do it, but for what reason? The right reason! Just because you do it does not mean that you have reached maturity, have everything mastered, or doing it for the right reason. Sometimes we do it and we talk to ourselves so that we can get into the right attitude. Every time I hear myself say something, it drives that statement deeper into my awareness. So there are times that we do something, but we do it even though we are battling something inside our attitude. Next time it will not be so hard to do it. What your hands find to do, do it (Ecclesiastes 9:10).

It is kind of like when we miss God, the first time it really bothers us, but the next time is does not bother us as much, and then soon we do it and think nothing of it. We are creatures of habit.

Eliezer has many gifts that are on those ten camels, but he picks out two particular gifts that he is going to give the bride right now as soon as she proves her willingness to do what needs to be done. In addition, this has nothing to do with the physical but the spiritual aspects.

Genesis 24:21,22 And the man wondering at her held his peace, to wit whether the Lord had made his journey prosperous or not.And it came to pass as the camels had done drinking, that the man took a golden earring of half a shekel weight and two bracelets for her hands of ten shekels weight of gold;

Now he had other gifts that were not earrings or bracelets, but here at the well, she has passed the test.

Now the Holy Ghost hangs purity on her hearing and on her deeds...

Therefore, we are going to hang purity on the fact that she listened to the right heart and she did the right deeds.

Genesis 24:23,24,25 And said, whose daughter art thou? Tell me, I pray thee: is there room in thy Father's house for us to lodge in?

And she said unto him, I am the daughter of Bethuel the son of Milcah, which she bare unto Nahor.

She said moreover unto him, we have both straw and provender enough and room to lodge in.

Now we are going to step to the next test. We have been studying Abraham test after test. With each of these tests, he steps up higher and higher, gains more, and becomes more of an eternal position with God.

Nevertheless, it is with Rebekah – her hearing is pure and her deeds are pure.

Now she will receive the next test, Eliezer asks her, "Is there room at your house for me?"

Is there room at your house for the Holy Ghost?

The home is the next test.

Notice, Rebekah not only says there is room at my house for the Holy Ghost, (Eliezer) but there is room for the Ten Commandments (ten camels)!

Moreover, I want you to come to my house, I want you to bring the Ten Commandments to my house and we are going to take care of it.

Whose daughter is Rebekah?

She is the daughter of Bethuel (her father), and then he is the son of Milcah the wife. (Instead of going to the husband, it went to the woman or wife (the church, symbolically).

Bethuel is the son of Milcah, so he is giving us the order in which these things transpire in dealing with the Church and the children of the Church.

Here is another order of saints: they are at the house, taking it easy.

Therefore, we understand that Bethuel was mentioned but one time. When the Holy Ghost comes back to the house with the camels, it is always the mother and the brother. Rebekah's brother's name is Laban, who will be the father of Jacob's two wives. However, all of this has prophetic overtones in it. Eliezer and the ten camels have come to the house with Rebekah, and he is going to be confronted, not by the husband, but by the wife and the brother. The man is the principles, but the brother who was not out there working will not go as an order of the bride. Even though he plays a role in this thing, he will not go as the bride because he was at the house. He was taking it easy.

Rebekah comes to the house. Guess who comes out to meet the Holy Ghost?

Brother!

In addition, he says, "We are so glad to see you, and we are honored to have you in our church."

Where were you out there when people needed that living water?

Brother says, "Well, I mean after all I work in the Church."

The setting is now that Eliezer is at the house with the camels. Laban (brother) makes provisions for the camels at the house, and he invites Eliezer (Holy Ghost) in. However, notice this: Rebekah has passed the second test and now she will move on to the third test. Eliezer announces his purpose of being here: "I have come to get my master's son a bride. In addition, I want to take this woman, who has qualified herself. back with me."

The Mother (the Church) and the brother (the principles) said, "No, no, we want her to be his bride, but we do not want her to leave for ten days, (universal completion)."

Symbolically speaking here:

I do not want the bride out of the Church until this thing is all over. What are we going to do if the bride

Who Are the Sons of the Promise?

leaves the church before this thing is all over? How are we going to make it through the tribulations if the bride is not here to help us? They have carried us all the way, they have stood in the gap, they made up the hedge and taken care of the flock. I do not want them to leave here. So Laban and mom said, "No, no, I do not want you to leave here for ten days."

We do not want the bride to leave in the rapture. We want her to stay here as long as I have to stay here, and we want her here. This Church will see its greatest revival just very brief after the rapture.

The Holy Ghost (Eliezer) says to the old buddy at Church and to the Church, "It is not up to you!"

So then Eliezer said to Rebekah, "Your mother, brother and your daddy (though we do not hear much out of him) want you to stay right here

for ten days (universal completion), but I want you to go with me right now. Rebekah, what are you going to do?" She replied, "I am ready to go." When she said that, here came the rest of the gifts. The title wave hit her and she passed the final test! Each time she passed another test, she received another spiritual gift. Therefore, it is in our lives also. Now he has given her additional gifts.

Before Eliezer leaves, he gives gifts to the Mother and the brother.

Many spiritual gifts in the Church are going to be manifested after the bride leaves. because right now they are just taking it easy. But when those who are in leadership and are leading the

Church spiritually are gone, then necessity will demand of others to get serious and polish up their gifts and get them to be manifested while those ten days are being completed or the tribulations are rolling on. All of those spiritual dreams, goals, and thoughts that people have had, that have pushed in the background of their lives because of this that and the other will become in the forefront. They will gain total priority in our lives, and they will be utilized in the Church.

Therefore, Laban and Mother both will have gifts after we are gone.

Incidentally, Rebekah's maidens are Bride attendants. They are not the bride, they did not draw the water, they did not water the camels, but they are bride attendants and they are going to ride with her on those camels.

If Rebekah and her attendants would have been lined up over there when Isaac saw them for the first time, Isaac could have picked out his bride quickly, because she would be wearing the gifts that he gave. (The Bible does not tell us how many attendants Rebekah had. There could have bee six or ten of them.) Rebekah would have those gifts that he had sent. Gifts that God has sent to you and gifts that He sent to me will be pronounced in our lives. They will be visible in our lives; they will be in the forefront of our lives.

When Isaac walked up and looked at this lady here and said, "You do not have any thing that I gave you, neither do you nor you. Now here is the one that has what I sent, and she is my bride." Therefore, this is the scenario in this setting, and so we are going to pick up the last few verses in this 24th chapter of Genesis. It is very important to understand that his chapter will touch every one of our lives. The Bride-Hood Saints that have gone by the way of the grave will still be a part of the bride while the rest of the dead live not. So there is an order that will come out of the grave.

Example: Jesus' resurrection... when He was resurrected out of the grave, there were certain saints who were resurrected out of the grave around Jerusalem and were seen on the streets. But not all the saints were seen.

Who Are the Sons of the Promise?

(If all had come up, the city would have had standing room only.) There were certain saints who came out of the grave at His resurrection and were seen in the city of Jerusalem. Just because you go in the way of the grave, this will not keep you from being in the rapture and being a part of His bride.

Genesis 24:62,63 And Isaac came from the way of the well Lahai-roi; for he dwelt in the south country. And Isaac went out to meditate in the field at the even-tide: and he lifted up his eyes and saw and behold, the camels were coming.

In the evening time, Isaac went out to meditate about the bride. He was meditating that the camels are coming and the hour that all this would be consummated, and so he was not at the house. The marriage supper is not in the throne room of God.

Revelation 14:14,15 And I looked and behold a white cloud and upon the cloud one sat like unto the Son of Man, having on his head a golden crown and in his hand a sharp sickle. And another angel came out of the temple, crying with a loud voice to him that sat on the cloud, Thrust in thy sickle and reap: for the time is come for thee to reap; for the harvest of the earth is ripe.

Jesus Christ is sitting on a cloud. I would like to talk about the second heaven, which is the cloud of witnesses. He is there with them, and they were purchased with his blood.

So, in this setting here, Jesus is not in the temple, He is sitting on a cloud.

Isaac was not in Abraham's tent; he was in the field meditating.

"And another angel came out of the temple and said unto him that sat upon the cloud, 'Thrust in thy sickle and reap, for the time of the harvest has come.'"

Now this is the parallel between Genesis 24:63 and Revelation 14:14-15.

Isaac is out in the field meditating;

Jesus is out sitting on the cloud…

Isaac is meditating about the bride;

Jesus' eyes are ever upon us, the Bride of Christ.

Now Jesus has on His head a crown (Revelation 14:14) – a single crown, a victor's crown – and He has conquered death, hell, and the grave. He has a single crown. When He comes back, many crowns are on His head (Revelation 19). (Many people confuse His appearing and His coming back.)

Revelation 19:12 His eyes were as a flame of fire and on his head were many crowns; and he had a name written that no man knew, but himself.

However, this is Revelation 14; this is a scenario of the rapture, the first catching away. If you read further, you will see that another one took place, but this is the first one.

Therefore, Jesus is sitting on the cloud with a cloud of witnesses (Hebrews 12:1). He is with His redeemed saints sitting there, but He has a crown. He has conquered, death, hell, and the grave. In his hand is a sharp sickle. He is ready for the harvest and ready for the rapture. That sharp sickle means that I am ready.

Revelation 1:13 And in the midst of the seven candlesticks one like unto the Son of Man, clothed with a garment down to the foot, and girt about the paps with a golden girdle.

Now only when one is ready for action is one girded about. If you are not ready for action, you just let everything hang free and enjoy the cool breeze. However, when you are ready for action, you gird yourself about as in Revelation 1:13 when He was girded about. In Revelation 14:14, He had a sharp sickle in his hand. He is ready. I believe if we could see him, he is sitting there and has that crown and sickle and is ready to hear the angel. The Bible says that no man knows the day or the hour of this rapture, not even Christ or the angels.

That is the reason in Revelation 14:14, He was sitting on the cloud and the angel came out from before God's throne and said to Him, "Thrust in the sickle." Jesus is ready, but the Father has not given Him the word.

Now it was at evening time, and friends this thing is about over.

There were 1500 years from the giving of the law to Christ on the cross.

God has given us 2000 years, and we will get into more of this in the Tabernacle study. It has been 2000 years from the cross to here, and it is evening time. It is evening time on this earth!

Where do you think that the enemy has the strong holds? Why?

It is in Syria, Iraq, and Iran.

This is exactly the place that God said, 3000 years ago, that the Anti-Christ would come from. We are in the evening time of this thing; the camels are coming and we need to be ready. God's camels, God's commandments, God's Word will be fulfilled.

Somewhere between Revelation 14:14 and Revelation

19:12, Jesus has been crowned King of Kings and Lord of Lords. Somebody has given him a multitude of crowns. He did not have them in the 14th chapter.

So Isaac has not received his bride. It is evening time; it is time that she should be coming in, and he is out there meditating about this.

We understand that Isaac lifted up his eyes...for he was watching...

Therefore, Jesus will be coming for those that are watching...

Genesis 24:64,65 And Rebekah lifted up her eyes and when she saw Isaac she lighted off the camel. For she had said unto the servant, what man is this that walketh in the field to meet us? And the servant had said it is my master: therefore she took a veil and covered herself.

Rebekah sees Isaac and Isaac sees Rebekah! He sees the camels coming, and says that is the Holy Ghost and his Bride. They were looking for each other; she ran to meet him. Eliezer in reality was older than Isaac, but he called Isaac "Master." Isaac was a type of Christ. Our master Jesus paid the price, and one day we will see Him also.

Genesis 24:66,67 And the servant told Isaac all things that he had done. And Isaac brought her into his mother Sarah's tent, and took Rebekah and she became his wife; and he loved her: and Isaac was comforted after his mother's death.

Eliezer the servant told Isaac all things. There is coming a judgment seat of Christ. We shall all stand before the judgment seat of Christ. All things will be revealed in your labor in the kingdom of God. Every good deed that you have done will be brought forward and you will receive a reward for it. Every time you have gone the second mile, every time that you drew another bucket of water, every time that you made a commitment that was beyond the call of duty, and every time that you did something in total servitude unto the Holy Ghost and the camels, you will receive a reward for it.

The Bible tells us that Isaac brought Rebekah to Sarah's tent.

Why did he not bring Rebekah to Abraham's tent?

Sarah has been dead awhile, but Isaac never took her to Abraham's tent. Rather he took her to Sarah's tent. He took her in commemoration of the church, in celebration of the church, in recognition of the church, in honor of the church. It is the church that the gates of hell cannot stand against. Therefore, the Marriage Supper of the Lamb is going to take place in the midst of the church. Blessed and holy is he that is called to the Marriage Supper of the Lamb. We are blessed!

The Holy Ghost is going to have more to do with the marriage supper than the Church world realizes, and we need to take heed. The Holy Ghost is so very important in our lives today and the Church will find its proper place and the place that God had ordained and intended for it to be.

Genesis 25:7,9,10,11 (in-part) And these are the days of the years of Abraham's life which he lived, a hundred threescore and fifteen years. And his sons Isaac and Ishmael buried him in the cave of Machpelah. There was Abraham buried and Sarah his wife. And it came to pass after the death of Abraham, that God blessed his son Isaac; and Isaac dwelt by the well Lahai-roi.

Abraham the great patriarch lived to be 145 years and

was buried with Sarah his wife. God blessed Isaac, the son of the promise.

Contact Information

Don Reed
PO Box 744
Sand Springs, OK 74063

www.WeDoBooksNow.com